All Art is Ecological

All Art is Ecological

TIMOTHY MORTON

PENGUIN BOOKS — GREEN IDEAS

PENGUIN BOOKS

UK | USA | Canada | Ireland | Australia
India | New Zealand | South Africa

Penguin Books is part of the Penguin Random House group of companies
whose addresses can be found at global.penguinrandomhouse.com.

First published in Penguin Books 2018
This extract published in Penguin Books 2021

005

Text copyright © Timothy Morton, 2018

Set in 11.5/14pt Dante MT Std
Typeset by Jouve (UK), Milton Keynes
Printed and bound in Great Britain by Clays Ltd, Elcograf S.p.A.

The authorized representative in the EEA is Penguin Random House Ireland,
Morrison Chambers, 32 Nassau Street, Dublin D02 YH68

A CIP catalogue record for this book is available from the British Library

ISBN: 978–0–141–99700–1

www.greenpenguin.co.uk

Penguin Random House is committed to a
sustainable future for our business, our readers
and our planet. This book is made from Forest
Stewardship Council® certified paper.

Contents

And You May Find Yourself Living in an Age of Mass Extinction

Exactly what is the current state of play, ecologically speaking? Let's explore this first. When I've told some people about the title of this essay, they have accused me of being weak. That's right: this essay is really lame. Some people wanted me to say 'You ARE Living in an Age of Mass Extinction,' as if the 'You may' was the same as 'You are not'.

This in itself is interesting, this understanding of 'may' as 'not'. It has to do with the logical 'Law' of the Excluded Middle. It affects all kinds of areas of life. The normal rule for voting interprets abstaining as saying 'No' when it comes to counting up the votes. You can't interpret it to mean 'Maybe yes, maybe no'. We live in an indicative age, an active one indeed, where a wordprocessing program is prone to punish you with a little wavy green line for using the passive voice; heaven forbid we use the subjunctive, as in 'you might'.

Not being able to be in the middle is a big problem for ecological thinking.

But not being able to be in the subjunctive is also a big problem for ecological thinking. Not being able to be in 'may' mode. It's all so black and white. And it edits out something vital to our experience of ecology, something we can't actually get rid of: the hesitation quality, feelings of unreality or of distorted or altered reality, feelings of the uncanny: feeling *weird*.

The feeling of not-quite-reality is exactly the feeling of being in a catastrophe. If you've ever been in a car crash, or in that minor catastrophe called jet lag, you probably know what I mean.

Indeed, editing out 'may' edit out experience as such. 'You ARE' means that if you don't feel like it, if you don't feel something officially sanctioned about ecology, there's something wrong with you. It should be transparent. It should be obvious. We should deliver this obviousness in an obvious way, like a slap upside the head. 'You may find yourself in' includes experience. In a sense, it's actually much *stronger* than a simple assertion. Because you can't get rid of yourself. You can agree or disagree with all kinds of things – there you are, agreeing or disagreeing. In the words of that great phenomenologist Buckaroo Banzai, *Wherever you go, there you are.*

Philo-sophy

There is something rough and ready about truth, just as there is something rough and ready about philosophy. Philosophy means *the love of wisdom*, not wisdom as such. It's definitely a style of philosophy to delete the *philos* part. There are too many philosophers to mention, and I blush to name them, but you know the type: the kind of person who *knows they are right* and that *you are talking nonsense unless you agree with them*. Needless to say, this is a style I don't like at all. Love means you can't and don't grasp the beloved – that's what you feel, that's what you realize when you love someone or something. 'I can't quite put my finger on it . . . I just love that painting . . .'

Throughout these pages, we'll be seeing how the experience of art provides a model for the kind of coexistence ecological ethics and politics wants to achieve between humans and nonhumans. Why is that?

In the late eighteenth century the great philosopher Immanuel Kant distinguished between things and thing-data. One reason why you can tell there is a sharp distinction here, argued Kant, is beauty, which he explored as an experience, the kind of moment in which we exclaim 'Wow, that's so beautiful!' (What I'm going to be calling 'the beauty experience'.) That's because beauty gives you a fantastic, 'impossible' access to the inaccessible, to the withdrawn, open qualities of things, their mysterious reality.

Kant described beauty as a feeling of ungraspability: this is why the beauty experience is beyond concept. You don't eat a painting of an apple; you don't find it morally good; instead, it tells you something strange about apples in themselves. Beauty doesn't have to be in accord with prefabricated concepts of 'pretty'. It's strange, this feeling. It's like the feeling of having a thought, without actually having one. In food marketing there is a category that developed in the last two decades or so called *mouthfeel*. It's a rather disgusting term for the texture of food, how it interacts with your teeth and your palate and your tongue. In a way, Kantian beauty is *thinkfeel*. It's the sensation of having an idea, and since we are so committed to a dualism of mind and body – so was Kant – we can't help thinking this is a bit psychotic: ideas shouldn't make a sound, should they? But we do talk all the time about the *sound* of an *idea: That sounds good.* Is it possible that there is some kind of truth in this colloquial phrase?

The German philosopher Martin Heidegger is a

controversial figure, because for some of his career he was a member of the Nazi party. This very dark cloud is a big shame, because it prevents many people from engaging with him seriously. And this is despite the fact that Heidegger, like it or not, wrote the manual on how thinking should proceed in the later twentieth and early twenty-first centuries. I hope I'll be able to demonstrate this here, and in addition I hope I can show that Heidegger's Nazism is a big mistake – obviously, but also from the point of view of his very own thought.

Heidegger argues that there are so such things as truth and untruth, rigidly distinguished like black and white. You are always in the truth. You are always in some kind of more or less low resolution, low dpi jpeg version of the truth, some kind of common, public version, *truthiness* (to use American comedian Stephen Colbert's handy parodic term). I know the jpeg analogy doesn't work properly. No analogy works properly. The analogy of truth as more or less pixellated is itself more or less pixellated.

And beauty is truthy. Actually, since I'm not Kant I'm going to say that beauty isn't thinkfeel, it's *truthfeel*. If you want to use the language scientists now use you can say *truth-like*. We can criticize factoids, those (usually quite small) chunks of data that have been interpreted so as to appear truthful. We could say that they are misleading, but why can they be misleading at all? It's because somehow we don't always recognize false things as false. Which means that there isn't a thin or rigid true versus false distinction. In a strange way, *all* true statements are sort of truthy. There is not a sudden point or rigid boundary at which the truthy becomes actually true. Things are always a bit fumbly and stumbly. We are feeling our way around. Ideas sound good. Truthfeel. And you may find yourself living in an age of mass extinction.

The Phenomenon of the Anthropocene

The Anthropocene is the name given to a geological period in which human-made stuff has created a layer in Earth's crust: all kinds of plastics, concretes and nucleotides, for example, have formed a discrete and obvious stratum. The Anthropocene has now officially been dated as starting in 1945. This is an astounding fact. Can you think of another geological period that has such a specific start date? And can you think of anything more uncanny than realizing that you are in a whole new geological period, one marked by humans becoming a geophysical force on a planetary scale?

There have been five mass extinctions in the history of life on Earth. The most recent one, the one that wiped out the dinosaurs, was caused by an asteroid. The one before that, the End Permian Extinction, was caused by global warming, and it wiped out all but a few lifeforms. Extinctions look like points on a time line when you look them up on Wikipedia – but they are actually spread out over time, so that while they are happening it would be very hard to discern them. They are like invisible nuclear explosions that last for thousands of years. It's our turn to be the asteroid, because the global warming that we cause is now bringing about the Sixth Mass Extinction. Maybe it would make it more obvious if we stopped calling it 'global warming' (and definitely stopped calling it 'climate change', which is really weak) and started calling it 'mass extinction', which is the net effect.

Now it may sound strange, but something about the vagueness of kinda sorta finding yourself in the Anthropocene, which is the reason why the Sixth Mass Extinction event on planet Earth is now ongoing – something about that vagueness is in fact *essential* and *intrinsic* to the fact of being in such an age. This is like saying that jet lag tells you something true about how things are. When you arrive in a very distant strange place, everything seems a little uncanny: strange, yet familiar, yet familiarly strange – yet strangely familiar. The light switch seems a little closer than normal, a little differently placed on the wall. The bed is oddly thin and the pillow isn't quite what you're used to – I'm describing how it feels whenever I arrive in Norway, by the way. Day begins about 10 a.m. during winter. It's pitch dark at 9 a.m. It's still the day, but not quite as you have become habituated to it.

Heidegger's word for how light switches seem to peer out at you like minor characters in an Expressionist painting is *vorhanden,* which means present-at-hand. Normally things kind of disappear as you concentrate on your tasks. The light switch is just part of your daily routine, you flick it on, you want to boil the kettle for some coffee – you are stumbling around, in other words, stumbling around your kitchen in the early morning light of truthiness. Things kind of disappear – they are *merely* there; they don't stick out. It's not that they don't exist at all. It's that they are less weird, less oppressively obvious versions of themselves. This quality of how things seemingly just happen around us, without our paying much attention, is telling us something about how things are: things aren't directly, constantly present. They only appear to be when they malfunction or are different versions of the same thing than we're used to. According to this, you go about your business in the Norwegian hotel room, you go to sleep, and when you wake up, everything is back to normal – and that's how things actually are; they are, as Heidegger says, *zuhanden*, ready-to-hand or handy. You have a grip on them, as in the phrase *Get a grip!* Or the slightly more amusing English version, *Keep your hair on!* (Implying before you quite notice that you are wearing a wig . . .)

Things are present to us when they stick out, when they are malfunctioning. You're running through the supermarket hell bent on finishing your shopping trip, when you slip on a slick part of the floor (someone used too much polish). As you slip embarrassingly towards the ground, you notice the floor for the first time, the colour, the pattern, the material composition – even though it was supporting you the whole while you were on your food shop mission. Being present is secondary to just sort of happening, which means, argues Heidegger, that *being isn't present*, which is why he calls his philosophy deconstruction or destructuring. What he is destructuring is the metaphysics of presence, which is saying that some things are more real than others, and the way they are more real is that they are more constantly present.

Normal for Some, Disaster for Others

This normalization is true – it happens, maybe it does have something to do with sleeping in a place. But is that really because things being handy, *zuhanden*, is the normal state of affairs? I adhere to a philosophical view known as *object-oriented ontology* (OOO), first formulated by an American philosopher, Graham Harman. OOO argues that nothing can be grasped, or accessed, all at once in its entirety. OOO also argues that thought is not the only access mode, and that thought is by no means the top access mode – indeed, *there is no top access mode*. What these two insights give us is a world in which anthropo-centrism is impossible, because thought has been extremely closely correlated with being human for so long, and because human beings have mostly been the only ones allowed to access other things in a meaningful way. OOO offers us a marvellous world in which being a badger, nosing past whatever it is that you, a human being, are looking at thought-fully, is just as validly accessing that thing as you are. This might be useful in an era during which we have come to know much more about ecology, and need to at least recognize the importance of other lifeforms. Anyway, when it comes to things being *zuhanden*, OOO is arguing that this ready-to-hand-ness of things is sitting on top of something much deeper and much stranger. There is a weird dislocation between *readiness to hand* and *presence at hand*. Stuff happens without us paying much attention (readiness to hand), yet the same stuff looks peculiar when it malfunctions (presence at hand). This is because things in themselves are ungraspable, totally and completely – irreducibly as they say. Things can't be accessed fully by anything, including themselves. You can flick a light switch, lick it, ignore it, think about it, melt it, fire its protons around a particle accelerator, write a poem about it, meditate upon it until you become Buddha. None of these will exhaust the reality of the switch. The switch could become sentient and develop the power of speech and go on a chat show. What it says on the show wouldn't be the switch – it would be switch autobiography. 'Well, I found myself in the fingers of this philosophy guy, he had jet lag, it was really weird . . . I had a difficult birth.'

Even the light switch would probably say something like the singer David Byrne in 'Once in a Lifetime' if it ever went on Oprah Winfrey's chat show: 'This is not my beautiful house . . .' And this is because things are mysterious, in a radical and irreducible way. *Mysterious* comes from the Greek *muein*, which means to close the lips. Things are unspeakable. And you discover this aspect of things, as if you could somehow *feel* that un-feelability, in the beauty experience, or as Keats puts it, *the feel of not to feel it*. This 'and you may find yourself' tentative hesitant subjunctive quality isn't just a temporary blip and it certainly isn't just a phenomenon that only occurs to sentient beings, let alone conscious ones, let alone human ones. It's sort of everywhere, because *being isn't presence*.

Kant showed that there's a difference between *the real* and *reality*. It's like the difference between a musical score – a bunch of dots and lines on a page – and the 'realization' of that score by a musician and the audience who showed up to hear it. Reality is, if you like, the *feeling* that it's real: the music is what it is – this is a Bach violin sonata, not a piece of electronic dance music – but it doesn't really 'exist' until you play it or listen to it.

Kant suggests that this 'realizer' is the 'transcendental subject', a rather abstract, universal being that's different from little me, but which seems to follow me around like an invisible balloon, 'positing' things as large or small, fast or slow (it's a pretty boring balloon, only in charge of extension in time and space). Since Kant, a number of other candidates for the 'realizer' have been suggested. Hegel argues that the 'realizer' was what he calls 'Spirit', the grand march of Western human history. Marx argues that it's human economic relations: sure, there are potatoes, but they don't really exist until I've dug one up and turned it into French fries. Nietzsche asserts that it's 'will to power': things are real because you say they are, and you're holding a rifle, so I'm not going to argue.

And Heidegger argues that it's a mysterious being called *Dasein*. The word is German for 'being there', and it's deliberately vague. Heidegger argues that more specific things (such as Kant's 'subject' or the concept of a human or of 'economic relations') are 'modes' of Dasein, a bit like musical key signatures. Ancient Mesopotamia is Dasein in the key of agricultural 'civilization', while the Aborigines are Dasein in the key of Paleolithic hunter-gatherers. Humans don't 'have' Dasein, because Dasein *produces* or *realizes* the human, in the same way that our violinist realizes the Bach sonata. And while there's nothing to suggest that Dasein can't be exclusively human, this is exactly the assertion that Heidegger blunders into. Dasein isn't quite there, constantly – it's a flickering lamplight. But for Heidegger it's exclusively human, and German flickering light is much more authentic than other kinds of flickering light. None of this makes sense. None of it makes sense *on*

Heidegger's own terms. This is what OOO is arguing. De-Nazifying Heidegger doesn't mean ignoring him or bypassing him. De-Nazifying Heidegger actually means *being more Heideggerian than Heidegger.*

So if the *truthfeel* of beauty is telling you something true about anything at all – anything at all is called *objects* in OOO, and these sorts of object are sharply different from objectified things, because they are radically mysterious – what truthfeel is telling you is that things are *open.* Also, the beauty experience is telling you that this thing, this thing I can see right here, is ungraspable. It's totally vivid, yet I can't get a grip on it . . . I can't keep my hair on at all. It's like what an American car wing mirror is telling you, out of the corner of your eye: *OBJECTS IN MIRROR ARE CLOSER THAN THEY APPEAR.* Or it's like objects on a shelf by the artist Haim Steinbach. Things are intrinsically kinky, kooky, out of place – this out of place-ness isn't just a function of things breaking and malfunctioning and becoming *vorhanden.* What you experience in jet lag or inside a Haim Steinbach installation is precisely about exactly how things are.

What all this amounts to is that it's the *normalization of things* that is the distortion. A distortion of distortion. Being in a place, being in an era, for instance an era of mass extinction, is intrinsically uncanny. We haven't been paying much attention, and this lack of attention has been going on for about twelve thousand years, since the start of agriculture, which eventually required industrial processes to maintain themselves, hence fossil fuels, hence global warming, hence mass extinction.

Love, Not Efficiency

Restructuring or destructuring this logistics of the world that has grown out of agriculture, which elsewhere I've called *agrilogistics,* is the one thing that would end global warming, but it is usually considered out of bounds, because it implies accepting a non-'modern' view. Agrilogistics means the logistics of the dominant mode of agriculture that started in Mesopotamia and other parts of the world (Africa, Asia, the Americas) around 10, 000 BGE. Agrilogistics has an underlying logic to do with survival: Neolithic humans needed to survive (mild) global warming, and so they settled in fixed communities that became cities, in order to store grain and plan for the future. They began to draw distinctions between the human and the non-human realms – what fits inside the boundary, and what exists outside of it – that continue to this day.

They also drew distinctions between themselves (the caste system). Very soon after the agrilogistical programme began, all kinds of phenomena we associate with life in general showed up, in particular patriarchy and social stratification, various kinds of class systems. It's important to remember that these are constructs of history, the consequence of nomads and hunter-gatherers settling down and establishing cities based on a certain form of survival mode.

The modern view was established on (although it thinks itself as a further disenchantment of) now ancient and obviously violent monotheisms, which in turn find their origin in the privatization of enchantment in the Neolithic with its 'civilization'.

Ecological awareness is awareness of unintended consequences. Some ecological politics is about trying to light everything up in a totally nonflickery way, to make sure that there are no unintended consequences. But this is impossible, because things are intrinsically mysterious. So an ecological politics like that would be a monstrous situation, a 'control society', a useful term invented by philosopher Gilles Deleuze to describe our contemporary world. An ecological control society would make the current state of affairs, where kids get tested every five seconds for their ability to resemble a rather slow computation device, look like an anarchist picnic. Even more predictability, even more efficiency. If that's what the ecological society to come will look like, then I really don't want to live in it. And it wouldn't even really be ecological. It would just be this same world, version 9.0.

The ecological society to come, then, must be a bit haphazard, broken, lame, twisted, ironic, silly, sad. Yes, sad, in the sense meant by a character in the British science fiction television series *Doctor Who*: sad is happy for deep people. Beauty is sad like that. Sadness means there's something you can't quite put your finger on. You can't quite grasp it. You have no idea who your boyfriend really is. This is not my beautiful wife. Which means in turn that beauty isn't graspable either, beauty as such – which means that beauty must be fringed with some kind of slight disgust, something that normative aesthetic theories are constantly trying to wipe off. There needs to be this ambiguous space between art and kitsch, beauty and disgust. A shifting world, a world of love, of *philos*. A world of seduction and repulsion rather than authority. Of truthiness rather than rigid true versus rigid false. Truth is just a 1000 dpi kind of truthiness. This isn't the same at all as saying everything is a lie. That's a statement that's trying not to be truthy, which is why it ends up contradicting itself. If everything is a lie, then the sentence *everything is a lie* must also be a lie . . . and so on.

Art That Talks about Its Substances

So we aren't talking about a traditional concept of postmodernity here. In a way, postmodern art, and I'd put Talking Heads' 'Once in a Lifetime' in that category, is in fact the beginning of ecological art, which is to say, art that includes its environment(s) in its very form. Of course, *all art is ecological*, just as all art talks in various ways about race, class and gender, even when it's not doing so explicitly. But ecological art is more explicit. Postmodernism may not have known it consciously at the time, but the ambient openness and strange distortedness of many of its forms talk about the Earth out of which they are ultimately made. Something real is happening. Extreme postmodern thought argues that nothing exists because everything is a construct. This idea, now known as *correlationism,* has been popular in Western philosophy for about two centuries. We just encountered it in our exploration of different kinds of 'realizer'. Again, the idea is that things in themselves don't exist until they have been 'realized', rather like the way a conductor might 'interpret' a piece of music or a producer might 'realize' a screenplay in a movie.

But something funny has happened to this idea. For reality to be correlationist, there has to be a correlatee as well as a correlator: there is a violin sonata, not just a violinist. It's like two faders on a mixing desk. Over time, the correlator fader has been turned way up, while the correlatee fader has been turned all the way down. And this has given rise to the actually rather boring (and definitely anthropocentric) idea that the world is exactly how humans make it, with the correlatee turned all the way down, so down that it sounds like the correlator is doing a solo, not a duet.

The lineage of correlationism starts with Kant, as we saw, who stabilized the explosive idea that causality can't be directly seen, only statistically inferred, the idea with which David Hume blew up pre-modern theories of cause and effect. Kant stabilized the explosion by saying that although causality can't be seen to be running forwards, it can be posited backwards with 20–20 hindsight by the correlator. Again, for Kant the correlator is what he calls the transcendental subject, and since Kant a number of alternatives have been suggested, as I mentioned earlier: the spirit of history (Hegel), human economic relations (Marx), will to power (Nietzsche), libidinal processes (Freud), Dasein (Heidegger), to name a few.

Correlationism is true: you can't grasp things in themselves, facts are different from data, and data is different from things. But that doesn't mean that what gets to decide what's real – the correlator, the decider – is more real than those things, whether the decider is the Kantian subject, Hegelian history, Marxist relations of human production, Nietzschean will to power, or Heidegger's flickering lamplight of Dasein. So while 'traditional' postmodernism, informed by Kant, still relies on this correlational-ism, what I'm talking about here, and what underlies OOO, is the idea that this very relationship may not be what we think it is. It may not exist at all.

Dark Ecology

Things are open. Open also in the sense of potential – things can happen in an OOO world, because things aren't totally keyed to human lamplight, they aren't totally meshed together, because in that world nothing could happen, there would just be this completely locked together jigsaw that you could never take apart or put back together. Something happening in one specific place (say a feather falling on pavement) would mean the whole universe changes every-where. Things are connected but in a kinda sorta subjunctive way. There's room for stuff to happen. Or, as the anarchist composer John Cage put it, 'The world is teeming. Anything could happen.'

So, the strangeness with which we encounter the fact that we are responsible for a mass extinction event is an intrinsic part of it, and not to be deleted. Yelling at people that we are making lifeforms go extinct isn't nice, because it deletes the strangeness. And saying conversely 'Who cares? Everything goes extinct anyway', which is sort of what the right wing often says, and also what some extreme forms of supposedly environmentalist stance say, such as eco-logical thinker Paul Kingsnorth's Dark Mountain project, isn't nice either, because that also tries to delete the strangeness. This kind of bleak certainty misses how things are.

My approach to ecological thought can be char-acterized as something I call 'dark ecology'. Dark ecology doesn't mean the absolute absence of light. It's more like Norway in the winter, or the summer for that matter, the way that light in the Arctic reveals something slippery and evanescent about itself, the long summer shadows, the night that lasts for fifteen minutes in Helsinki in June, the dimness. Light as such isn't directly present, you can't pin it down and you can't fully illuminate it: what illuminates the illuminator? Light is splashy and blobby, as quantum theory tells us. And it can't reach everywhere all at once, as relativity theory tells us.

It's like when you die in Tibetan Buddhism. When you die, you see the light – but unlike in some other religions, it's not an obvious light and it's not at the end of a tunnel, and you aren't heading towards it and it isn't the end. In fact, you probably don't notice it at all. It just sort of flickers on, in an incidentally by-the-way sort of a way, and you delete that experience of the nature of mind, then you find yourself being reincarnated. In the traditional literature it lasts for about three seconds, or as the esoteric manuals put it, as long as it takes you to stick your arm into a sleeve three times. You are not deleting some constantly present logos and falling into blurry confusion. In a way you are deleting a wonderful blurry confusion and falling into a fatal certainty.

In Tibetan Buddhism, the time between one life and the next is called the bardo, the 'between'. All kinds of haunting images appear to the consciousness in that state, images based on past actions (karma). We feel that things are different now, that we are in a bardo-like transition space regarding

ecological awareness. But really what we are notic-
ing is that things just don't stay put, they don't stay
the same. Trying to get over this bardo-like quality
results in damage to lifeforms, damage to thinking,
damage to experience. The impulse behind racism,
for example, is also what empowers a thin and rigid
distinction between humans and nonhumans. The
violence has already occurred, in the form of the
abjection and dehumanizing of some humans. We
humans contain nonhuman symbionts as part of the
way in which we are human; we couldn't live without them. We are not human all the way through.
We and all other lifeforms exist in an ambiguous
space in between rigid categories.

If ecological action means *not doing as much
damage,* rather than doing things more efficiently,
then it's not ecological to insist or slap upside the
head or the other similar current modes of supposedly ecological data delivery in general. These
kinds of action are like trying to wake us up from
this bardo-like dream – but the dreamlike quality
is precisely what is most real about ecological reality, so in effect, throwing out factoids and statistics
in information dump mode is making ecological
experience, ecological politics and ecological philosophy utterly impossible.

Thinking about Groups

Humans have started mass extinction, but me, little me, Tim Morton, and little you, didn't do anything. Once again, nothing, nothing that you did, such as starting your car, has had a statistically meaningful effect. Yet billions of car startings and burstings of coal into flame and so on totally have had an effect. There is an uncanny gap between little me and me as a member of what is called *species*. The human species caused global warming, not the octopus species, let's be very clear about that. But species is exactly what you can't point to. I find that I am and I am not a human, insofar as I did and did not contribute to global warming, depending on what scale you think I'm on, so these scales don't have a smooth transition point between being one human and being part of the total population of humans – suddenly we find ourselves on one scale or another. It's that paradox again. And it seems absurd. Surely seven billion (the current human population) is just one human times seven billion? In computational terms, there is total smoothness between one and seven billion. Yet there is a weird gap.

If you think metaphysically, you can apply a sorites logic to global warming. The sorites paradox is the logical paradox concerning heaps. It's about how vague heaps are – when does a collection of things become a heap? If you take a single rock away from a heap of rocks, does that mean it is no longer a heap? What if you take ten rocks away? Where does the heap start, and where does it end? This quandary suggests a great deal of vagueness, and some philosophers don't like vagueness, so they don't believe heaps exist at all. The trouble is, ecological things such as populations (for example human ones) and ecosystems are very well described as heaps of things. So we had better allow heaps to exist if we're going to be ecological, because addressing global warming and mass extinction can only be done at a massive, *collective* scale.

If you think about it, global warming is a *heap* of actions. Let's analyse it using the logic that results in the sorites paradox. One car ignition firing doesn't cause global warming. Two? No. Three? No. You can work your way all the way to one billion and the same logic will hold. So there is no global warming. Or – drum roll – your logic sucks. How does it suck? It sucks by having no time for things that are in between true and false, black and white. Ecological beings such as lifeforms and global warming require *modal* and *paraconsistent* logics. These logics allow for some degree of ambiguity and flexibility. Sentences can be *kind of* true, *slightly* false, *almost* right.

Heidegger argues that 'true' and 'false' aren't so rigidly different as you might think. You can't delete truthiness without getting into trouble, as I showed a bit earlier, because 'true' applies to the things that Dasein is concerned with, and Dasein is mysterious and slippery. So we are always in the truth, because *Dasein is the truth* we keep trying to seek outside of Dasein. We're always entangled in a thicket of prefabricated concepts that might not apply so well, because of the slippery quality of being. Perhaps this is why social media can be so violent: on Twitter, for example, everyone is trying to be right in one hundred and forty characters or less. Anxieties about 'fake news' exist because in some ways, all news is 'fake'. Everyone is trying to contain or erase the truthiness. But if entities are open, they are not completely nothing, nor are they constantly present, nor are they reducible to other things such as their parts or some access mode such as discourse or economic relations or Dasein. If entities are open, they are truthy through and through. And this actually implies that you can't say just anything you want about entities. You can't say an octopus is a toaster, or that global warming isn't real, or that it wasn't caused by humans, precisely *because* things are open and truthy. Things are exactly what they are, yet never how they appear, yet appearance is inseparable from being, so a thing is a twisted loop like a Möbius strip, in which the twist is everywhere, it has no starting or ending point. Appearance is the intrinsic twist in being.

An agricultural person – aka us – realizing that she is in a twisted historical or ethical or philosophical space experiences what is called tragedy, which is an agricultural-age way of computing the damage caused by an agricultural age. I'm caught in a twisted loop in which my attempt to escape the web of fate has been but a further entwining of that web. Tragedy supposes that looping is evil and that despite the fact that you find you can't escape fate, especially when you try, there is this forlorn hope that in the end, or in some better world over yonder that we can never reach, we might be able to slip those bonds once and for all, hence the ultimately religious horizon of tragedy, where for instance the chorus tells you that there is nothing here that is not Zeus (in ancient Greek playwright Euripides' play *Heracles*).

Tragedy is in fact a small region of comedy space, which is twisted all the way through. Right now, ecological awareness presents itself as tragedy. But sooner or later, we will start to smile, which is maybe how we get to cry for real. Since there is no beyond in which things are indeed totally straight, totally untwisted, it's funny to watch us as a species acting as if there was such a beyond, and constantly slipping into the web of fate, like a slapstick character whose attempt to get from A to B keeps being hampered by his very style of trying to get from A to B. This is why art, which disables getting from A to B by causing the illusion of smooth functioning to malfunction, so as to reveal the spooky openness of things, is in the end joyful and funny, though we need to traverse and respect and not delete a realm of exquisite pain to get there. We really are making this Earth unlivable for ourselves and other lifeforms. I'm not suggesting we just sit back and laugh at that.

Several realms, in fact. Realms of truthfeel. Ecologically speaking, I think the pathway is likely to lead us from guilt down into shame, and from there down into disgust, whence to horror; from there begins ridicule, which dies out in melancholia, whose enabling chemistry is sadness; in turn, sadness is conditioned by longing, which implies joy. At present, the ways in which we talk to ourselves about ecology are stuck in horror mode: disgust, shame, guilt. Eventually things get so horrifying that someone goes 'You gotta be fucking kidding', like that character in John Carpenter's film *The Thing*, looking at the latest mutation of the feminized simulation monster. A ridiculous, absurd laughter breaks out. We aren't quite there yet – we're almost there, which is why some really progressive ecological art, such as the work of the American artist Marina Zurkow, plays with a sardonic kind of eco-humour. We are beginning to trust the tactic of not waking ourselves up from the nightmare, but allowing ourselves to fall further into it, beyond horror. Underneath ridicule space is a melancholy region where things become less horrifying and more uncertain, all kinds of fantasy beings float around like mermaids among the seaweed and submarines. A realm of unspeakable, nonhuman beauty not confined to normative anthropocentric parameters begins to open up.

Another way of saying the same thing is that we are starting to trust that we are in a *catastrophe,* which literally means a space of downward-turning. It's much better to think you are in a catastrophe than to think you are in a disaster. There are no witnesses in disaster. Disasters are what you witness from the outside. Catastrophes involve you, so you can do something about them.

Think about it. This whole 'world without us' fantasy is very suspicious from that point of view. In the last two decades, philosophers and television producers and artists have taken an interest in imagining an Earth without humans. I'm not sure exactly why it started, but I'm pretty sure of the general reason: the media is tuning in to global warming and mass extinction. The paradox is that as you imagine a future in which humans have gone extinct, *there you are, imagining that*. It's a vicarious thrill, like rubbernecking a car accident, and it might be just as obnoxious and dangerous. In the real world, given how entangled we have become with earth systems, if we go extinct it means that many, many lifeforms have also gone extinct or are about to. Opposing anthropocentrism doesn't mean that we hate humans and want ourselves to go extinct. What it means is seeing how we humans are included in the biosphere as one being among others.

This brings up a deep philosophical insight about the fact that we simply can't be on the outside looking in. Scientists call this fact 'confirmation bias' and philosophers call it 'the hermeneutic circle' and 'phenomenological style'. There is no way to escape such things. How I interpret data will depend on what I think I want to find. How I see myself depends on the kind of person I am. How I interpret things is entangled with prefabricated concepts about what interpreting means. This gives rise to a strange insight, which is that living in a scientific age doesn't mean you are living in a cold world of objectivity. It means that you realize you can't achieve escape velocity from your phenomenological style or embeddedness in data interpretation or confirmation bias (three different ways of saying the same thing). We cannot get out.

Funnily enough, living in a scientific age means we have stopped believing in authoritative truth. That kind of truth is pretty medieval, always backed up by the threat of violence because it can't be proved: you just have to believe it. Instead, our modern age is a truthiness domain. Science means we still might be wrong, and we may find ourselves holding on to a bunch of weird assumptions that don't quite make sense, but this is better than firmly believing we are right because the Pope ordered us to believe whatever.

Mass extinction is so awful, so incomprehensible, so horrible – and at present it's so invisible. We hardly know where to start, apart from either ignoring it or electroshocking ourselves about it. One of the recent mass extinctions, the End Permian Extinction, also involved global warming. It happened about 252 million years ago, and at that time, plants were to blame. Unlike plants, we can choose not to emit excessive amounts of carbon, so it's not inevitable this time.

When I say *recent*, I'm alluding again to the fact there have only been five previous mass extinctions in the four-billion-year history of life on this planet. That fact alone, that fact of deep time, is horrifically disturbing. It was disturbing in the early nineteenth century, when geologists began to figure it out, and it's disturbing now. We used to tell ourselves that it was disturbing to the poor dumb Victorians because it shook their faith in God. In exactly what is it shaking our faith now?

Ecology without Nature

Ecological awareness is shaking our faith in the anthropocentric idea that there is one scale to rule them all – the human one. Nietzsche announced that God was dead in the nineteenth century, and this is often taken to imply that humans face a meaningless existence. But this isn't true. It's the opposite. The death of God isn't some empty, desolate wilderness, it's a scary jungle swarming with creatures – literally. It's thousands of equally legitimate spatiotemporal scales that have suddenly become available and significant to humans. We are so habituated to living and thinking on a very small range of timescales that students who train as geologists say that they have to go through a process of acclimatizing to much vaster tracts of time.

Now we know that ecological awareness means thinking and acting ethically and politically on a lot of scales, not just one. It's not true, however, that this will feel like the kind of powerful thrill you get from playing with one of those online scale tools that zoom you in and out from the Planck length (the smallest currently measurable one) to the scale of the entire universe, or those humbling-yet-empowering clock faces on which humans appear at the last second before midnight; or those floor diagrams some scientist presenter walks across to show how we appear at the last sliver on the bottom right-hand corner. The scale in all of those is smooth and consistent – it's a sort of hollowed-out, blown-up version of the good old anthropocentric scaling, only now we are in a privileged godlike position of omnipresence outside the universe, where every scale is just a toggle away. But it isn't like that at all. That kind of thing confuses time with the *measurement* of time, and further it confuses the measurement of time with just a *few* kinds of measurement – the kinds that are convenient for humans. It's not just true that there is a time for everything, as it says in Ecclesiastes ('a time to reap and a time to sow . . .'); it's the case that from grasses to gorillas to gargantuan black holes, *everything has its own time,* its own temporality.

Psychological research has shown that we are good at narrating the correct sequence of geological events: Earth emerges from a cloud of dust and gas, microbes evolve, followed by sponges, fish, butterflies, primates . . . But very few of us are able to imagine the right *durations* of geological time without special training. And being able to understand durations is particularly important for us right now, because global warming's effects may last up to 100,000 years. What does that actually mean? We tend to have only two vague temporal categories in our heads: ancient and recent. We use these as a template to conceptualize what we call 'prehistory' (the pre-'civilization' human stuff, and the nonhuman stuff) and 'history' (the 'civilization' stuff). It would be better, more logical and requiring fewer beliefs to see everything – even now – as history and to see history as not exclusively human.

I think we have more in common with the Victorians than we'd sometimes like to admit. Indeed, the decisive emergence of what I call *hyperobjects* on our radar makes the sensibility of our contemporary moment extremely Victorian. Mary Anning discovered a dinosaur skeleton in an English cliff face, and the abyss of deep time opened up. The vast distributed processes of evolution were discovered. The gigantic Pacific weather system El Niño was discovered later in the nineteenth century. Marx traced the invisible workings of capitalism. Freud discovered the unconscious. And once again we stand in awe of gigantic entities massively distributed in time and space, in such a way that we can only point to tiny slices of them at a time. Once again we find our faith shaken, and now it has clearer contours: it's not about the disappearance of an agricultural-age god. It's much, much worse. It's about the flip side, the unconscious, the unintended consequences of our faith in progress, which far precedes agricultural-age gods, as a matter of fact, and is their condition of possibility. A 12,500-year-long social, philosophical and psychic logistics is now showing its colours, and they are disastrous.

And for the longest time these logistics were called Nature. Nature is just agricultural logistics in slow motion, the nice-seeming buildup to the Anthropocene, the gentle slope of the upwardly moving rollercoaster that you don't even suspect to be a rollercoaster. Agricultural society coincided with the Holocene (our current geological period, which started over 10,000 years ago, marked by the retreat of the glaciers), which was remarkably stable and cyclic as far as Earth systems such as the nitrogen and carbon cycles went. It's controversial, but some geologists actually think that the periodic, smoothly cycling form of the Holocene was in fact a product of the functioning of a certain agricultural mode. This mode began in Mesopotamia and elsewhere on

Earth at the start of the Holocene. If it's true that agriculture contributed to the stability of Earth systems, it makes things even more disturbing. Like when someone has a seizure, and their brain waves become beautifully regular just beforehand. Or before an earthquake, when the same thing happens to the tectonic plates. On this view, what is called Nature – the smooth cycling represented so nicely in feudal symbolic systems – is directly the Anthropocene in its less obvious mode. Then comes the huge Earth systems data spike we see in the ex-American Vice President Al Gore's movie *An Inconvenient Truth*, the spike that starts around 1945, evidence of runaway carbon emissions. Everything starts to go haywire.

The inner logic of the smoothly functioning system – right up until the moment at which it wasn't smoothly functioning, aka now – consists of logical axioms that have to do with survival no matter what. Existence no matter what. Existing overriding any *quality* of existing – human existing that is, and to hell with the lifeforms that aren't our cattle (a term from which we get *chattels,* as in women in many forms of patriarchy, and the root of the word *capital*). Existence above and beyond qualities. This supremacy of existing is a default ontology and a default utilitarianism, and before any of it was philosophically formalized, it was built into social space, which now means pretty much the entire surface of Earth.

You can see it in the gigantic fields where automated farm equipment spins in its lonely efficient way. You can feel it in the field analogs such as huge meaningless lawns, massive parking lots, supersized meals. You can sense it in the general feeling of numbness or shock that greets the fact of mass extinction. Quite a while ago humans severed their social, philosophical and psychic ties with nonhumans. We confront a blank-seeming wall in every dimension of our experience – social space, psychic space, philosophy space.

Uncannily we begin to realize that we are somewhere. Not nowhere. And we may find ourselves living in an age of mass extinction. I'm all for letting us linger in the strange openness of this uncanny discovery that space was just a convenient white Western anthropocentric construct for navigating your way around Africa to reach the Spice Islands, and so on. Because strangely, this feeling of openness, this uncanny sensation of finding ourselves somewhere and not recognizing it, is exactly a glimpse of living less definitively, in a world comprised almost entirely not of ourselves.

Tuning

Let's think about the delivery mode of ecological advice – drive less, shop locally, save energy, all the usual 'shoulds' that we hear again and again. Either we are being preached to as individuals, being made to feel bad and encouraged to change our habits, so that maybe we will feel better, because we think others think of us differently – or we are being lectured at, made to feel powerless, because the thought of revolution or other big kinds of political change are very inspiring, but also bring up thoughts of how they might be resisted or constrained: the powers that be are too great, revolutions are always co-opted . . . Maybe they're just impossible on any scale that would matter. Sometimes I think, 'Really? I have to assemble a huge group of humans and start a revolution right now, *then* I can relate to polar bears?'

But awareness of the sensuous existence of other life-forms doesn't have to involve big ideas or actions.

How about just visiting your local garden centre to smell the plants?

Why this constant and very particular orientation to the future – what needs 'to be done' in order to start being ecological? It's a sort of gravity well that ecological thought about ethics and politics can get stuck in. You think *future* and you think *radically different from the present*. You think *I need to change my mindset, now, then I can really start making a difference*. You are thinking along the lines of agricultural religion, which is designed mostly to keep agricultural hierarchies in place. You are trying to get the right attitude towards some transcendent principle; in other words, you are operating within the language of good and evil, guilt and redemption. Agricultural religion (Judaism, Christianity, Hinduism and so on) is implicitly hierarchical: there's a top tier and a bottom one, and the very word *hierarchy* means *the rule of the priests*. By framing ecological action this way, you have been sucked into a gravity well, and it's not an especially ecological space down there. In many ways, it's not helping at all. For instance, there's really no reason to feel individual guilt: your individual actions are statistically meaningless.

We don't have to frame an ecological future as being radically different, at least not in quite that way. Now some of you may be tempted to close this book because you've already pegged me as a quiet-ist who doesn't want to address the elephants in the room such as neoliberal capitalism. You'd be quite wrong. I'm talking about exactly *how* to address the elephants, considering that all forms of elephant address so far haven't worked out so well for planet Earth (and all the creatures, including humans, who live on it). There's nothing wrong with being a little bit hesitant and thoughtful and reflective. But anti-intellectualism is the favourite hobby of . . . the intellectual. At the end of ecology conferences, you so often hear someone saying, 'But what are we going to *do?*' And this has to do with guilt about sit-ting on chairs for a few days thinking and talking (and perhaps also with the sheer physical frustration of sitting on chairs for a few days).

I want to take an entirely different approach. I want to persuade you that you are *already* being eco-logical, and that expressing that in social space might not involve something radically, religiously differ-ent. Don't think this means that nothing changes, that you are just the same when you know about being ecological. It's rather hard to describe what happens, but something does happen. It's like some-one slit your being with a very sharp and therefore imperceptible scalpel. You started bleeding every-where. It's something like that.

A couple of years ago, I was being interviewed for a magazine. The interviewer was asking a lot of devil's advocate type questions, so many in fact that I started to think that they weren't devil's advocate questions at all. I started to think that he seriously didn't like the idea of acting ecologically. I wondered how I was going to convince him. Then I wondered whether convincing mode was the best way of addressing his stance. As I've just described, this mode might have some bugs in it, bugs from religious discourses that were originally set up in part to justify a massive firewall between humans and nonhumans (cattle over here, frogs over there, cats charmingly – or suspiciously, perhaps – in the boundary space between here and there). And ecological action is very evidently about not having such a firewall.

Then something occurred to me.

'Do you have a cat?' I asked.

'Yes,' he replied, perhaps somewhat taken aback by the oblique and simple question.

'Do you like to stroke her or him?'

'Oh, yes of course.'

'Well, so you're already relating to a nonhuman being for no particular reason. You're already being ecological.'

The journalist didn't like it. Conventional wisdom says that being ecological is a special, different mode of being, akin to becoming a monk or a nun. And the theory of action that fuels this special being also has a religious patina to it, in an antiquated way. Let's consider a different approach altogether.

It's going to take us a little while to get the hang of the 'no particular reason' part of the above statement. And it's going to take a while to determine exactly what 'relating to' means. Both have to do with a concept that I'm going to call *tuning*. I think we are already being ecological – we just aren't consciously aware of it. And those of us who *say* they're being ecological might be saying it in a mode that doesn't have anything in particular to do with coexisting nonviolently with nonhuman beings, which is roughly what I take ecological ethics and politics to mean. This nonviolence doesn't have to be as extreme as Jainism, perhaps. And perhaps it can't pretend to be perfect or pure. It's fraught with ambiguities, because sharks can eat you and viruses can kill you and it would be a good idea to protect our human selves from viruses and sharks. Furthermore, we can't determine in advance how wide the net of our concern should be, because we don't know everything about all lifeforms, and we don't know how they are all interrelated – and our actions cause further interrelations, tangling us even more. Nonviolence in this respect is uneasy and shifting.

Free Will is Overrated

We have, incidentally, made some ethical and political progress in the last couple of pages, though you may not have noticed. One thing that we just got clear is that it's possible to combine traditional environmental ethics and politics with animal rights ethics and politics. Though they seem like they might be naturally akin, some people regard joining up these two discourses as an impossible task, like squaring the circle. Environmentalism and ecological science is often about populations rather than individuals, and populations are considered very differently from individuals – in ways, animal rights critics might argue, that are insensitive to specific nonhuman beings: how they can be managed and controlled, for example. Animal rights talk, on the other hand, is frequently concerned with specific individual lifeforms – how they suffer, how they should be treated – even if there are many of them. But the seeming difference in focus between these two types of thinking may not be as distinct as it seems, and it has to do with something we've been exploring, namely our trouble with thinking wholes and parts. Let's consider the sharp distinction between what is considered to be an environment (or ecosystem) and a lifeform (individual animal).

We think, for example, that ecosystems (and populations of lifeforms, for that matter) are wholes with parts that relate to them mechanically, in the sense that they are replaceable. If there's something wrong with your engine, you replace a component and it's fixed. Science is ethically neutral but you can imagine using ecological science to justify a certain kind of unpleasant ethics. A lifeform goes extinct? Never mind, the whole will generate a new component to take its place. You can imagine that this doesn't work very well for the animal rights crowd.

But we are also going to need to have a little conversation about rights. If the choice is between mechanical wholes and separate individuals defined according to the normal manuals for defining such things, I don't want anything to do with either. They might actually be two halves of a torn whole, as one philosopher, Theodor Adorno, liked to put this sort of thing. The trouble is that rights and citizenship and subject-hood (and languages related to those concepts) have to do with possessing things. Individual rights are based on property rights, so that *being in possession of yourself* is one criterion for having them, for example. But if everything has rights, nothing can be property, so nothing can have rights. It's as simple as that. Scaled up to Earth magnitude, rights language doesn't work at all. The other problem is that to grant someone rights, you traditionally have to show that the someone is indeed a someone, in other words, that such a being has a self-concept. So the poor chimpanzee, to take an example from American law, has to wait around until enough humans are kind enough to condescend to grant it a self-concept. So far, such an approach has not been working out so well for the chimpanzee – or most other nonhuman creatures either.

This is why what Ecuador did in response to the oil corporation Chevron was so fascinating. Thirty thousand Ecuadorians living in the Amazon rain-forest brought a $27 billion lawsuit against Chevron for drilling the Lago Agrio oil field, saturating the topsoil with viscous oil. From 2007 to 2008, Ecuador rewrote its constitution to allow for the 'rights of nature'. This means that the nonhuman world has the right to exist and regenerate. If you think this is dangerously anthropomorphic, then too bad. The problem is that there is no other way for us as humans to include nonhumans within rights language than to bring them under the human umbrella under which we are sheltering. The difficulty is, many of the tools we have for making correct decisions are contaminated in advance with anthropocentric chemicals, as we will see in the following paragraphs.

The division between *act* and *behave,* which is based on a medieval Neoplatonic Christian doctrine of soul and body, structures how we distinguish between ourselves (the ones we allow to *act*) and nonhumans (the ones we only believe to be *behaving,* like puppets or androids). But are *we* Neoplatonic Christian souls? Isn't being a person a little bit about being paranoid that you might *not* be a person? Can you get rid of the ambiguity without tearing something?

There is an additional issue. We observe some emotions in nonhumans such as elephants, but we are less willing to let elephants feel emotions that seem less 'useful' to us. We can let elephants be hungry when they look hungry, but we have trouble allowing that they are happy when they look happy. That, for some reason, would be anthropomorphic, and many environmentalist thinkers are concerned not to be, although I've argued that it's impossible, since even if you intend not to be, there you are, a human, relating in whatever human way you are relating to whatever other lifeform. It's interesting that we think that sheer survival (hence hunger) is more 'real' than some kind of quality of exist-ing (such as being happy). It says a lot about us that just surviving, being hungry, are supposedly 'real', aka nothing to do with being human in particular – what does that say about us and what does it in fact do to us ourselves, let alone the elephants? Ecological catastrophe has been wrought in the name of this survival, sheer existing without heed to any *quality* of existing. Objectively, in terms of how we have acted it out, this default utilitarianism has been very harmful to *us*, let alone other lifeforms. That says it all, doesn't it? It's like that language about the bottom line. We may feel bad about workers suffering, but profits must be maintained, corporations must go on existing for the sake of existing. These two types of thought – about survival and bottom lines – are synonymous.

The environmental approach could be described as taking care of the whole at the expense of individuals, while the animal rights approach could be described as taking care of individuals at the expense of the whole. We seem to be at an impasse. But notice a feature of the two approaches. The 'take care of the whole at the expense of the individuals' and the 'take care of the individuals at the expense of the whole' approaches do share something. They are trying to give you a good reason to care about nonhumans. But what if *having a good reason to care* was precisely a large part of the problem? Getting a bit more granular, animal rights and environmentalism give reasons that are reductionist. Reductionism doesn't necessarily mean that large things are made of small things that are more real than large things. Sometimes we can reduce small things to large things. The environmentalist approach defines wholes as more real than (and so more important than) their parts, or they describe parts as more real than (and so more important than) wholes.

We can start to break through this difficult impasse by noting that what is called *environment* is just lifeforms and their extended genomic expressions: think of spider's webs and beaver's dams. When you think this way, you are already thinking about wholes and parts in a different way.

And when you think of things like *that,* there's really no difference between thinking about what is called an ecosystem and what is called a single lifeform. Problem solved.

Thinking about wholes and parts in this way is a key component of good old-fashioned art appreciation theory. A work of art is a whole, and this whole contains many parts – the materials out of which it's made being just one of them. We could include the interprective horizons of the art's consumers, for example, and the contexts in which the art materials were assembled – a highly explosive concept, as we saw earlier. In this way it's obvious that there are so many more parts than there is whole. In an age of ecological awareness there is no one scale to rule them all. This means that art and art appreciation won't stay still, in the way that a lot of art theory (for instance in Kant) wants. And in the absence of a single authoritative (anthropocentric) standard of taste with which to judge art, how we regard it is also about how wholes are always less than the sums of their parts. A work of art is like a transparent bag full of eyes, and each eye is also a transparent bag full of eyes. There is something inherently weird, even disgusting, about beauty itself, and this weirdness gets mixed back in when we consider things in an ecological way. This is because beauty just happens, without our ego cooking it up. The experience of beauty itself is an entity that isn't 'me'. This means that the experience has an intrinsic weirdness to it. This is why other people's taste might come across as bizarre or kitschy.

The truth is the choice to be able to care or not care is always an illusion anyway. You are always in care space, always in truthiness (as in the previous essay). If you say 'I don't care about this issue,' it means that you care about this issue enough to say that. Often, in the real world, saying you don't care much about someone or something means you might be hiding that you care very much indeed.

Consider the phenomenon of 'single source recycling' where you don't have to sort stuff into plastics, cardboard, organic waste and so on: your bin cares about the recycling, so you don't have to. Some environmentalists have objected to it, visiting houses in my home town of Houston, Texas, for example, and persuading people to sign petitions. But why? Why the search for hypocrisies in the new process? Because it eliminates the idea of free will, and the performance of 'look at me I am doing good'. The idea that we're outside the world looking in, deciding from a menu which choice to make, is precisely the dangerous illusion.

When you play a game such as cricket or baseball, the ball arrives at your bat within a few milliseconds. That's faster than your brain. You can practise and practise so that you can hit that ball when it arrives. That sounds elementary. But if you think about the fact that the ball is still faster than your brain, what on Earth is happening? Whatever is happening is a direct refutation of the Neoplatonic Christian idea we are still retweeting, that we have a mind-like or soul-like thing that is somehow inside us like a gas in a bottle, totally different from that bottle in some way, and that it is a sort of puppet master pulling the strings. You think you are about to hit that ball, but you have already hit it. Free will, as I keep saying, is overrated.

But it's even more strange and interesting. Consider an actual scenario. The fastest cup-stacker on

Earth (a young boy) competed with David Eagleman, a neuroscientist, on his show, *The Brain*, which ran on PBS in America in 2015. They are wired up to brain scanners. The neuroscientist's brain is working overtime and he loses. The boy's brain is hardly working at all. It's as if he is a zombie. He isn't intending to stack the cups and there isn't a puppet master inside his head pulling the strings. Something else is happening. His ability to stack the cups is *all* in his 'body'. Is the brain more like some kind of starter, which gets things going, then sits back? Well, we've just refuted that – the feeling of having made a decision might arrive slightly *after* you've made it, whatever it is. So the brain isn't even that, some kind of prime mover of a mechanism that keeps going once you've pressed a button. It looks as if what we're observing is neither mechanical (the latter option) nor orchestral (the former one). Some boss doesn't start the machine, and some conductor doesn't need to 'intend' everything all the time – as any concert musician will tell you (my father, for example), the conductor is never actually driving the music like that anyway.

Both these models have to do with a myth. The myth is that for something to exist, it must be constantly present: the metaphysics of

THIS IS

NOT HERE

presence. The soul-and-body, 'conductor' model seems up to date because it has to do with management, ownership and all kinds of things associated with the notion of private property that influence a lot of what we do on this Earth. But this turns out, as we have seen, to be a retweet of a Neoplatonic Christian concept.

Furthermore, the 'on switch' model of action depends on a mechanical theory of causation that requires some kind of god-like being at the start of the causal chain, to get the ball rolling. After that, the ball hits the next ball in a mechanical way. So the mechanical theory is really just a variant or upgrade of the 'conductor' one. And this is therefore merely a modification of our Neoplatonic retweet: the soul is the driver, the body is the chariot . . .

Let's make a new word: *alreadiness*. This word is going to come in very handy, because now I don't have to resort to a suggestive but rather clunky phrase from one of my favourite philosophical regions: deconstruction. This would be the famous *always-already* employed by Heidegger and then by Jacques Derrida, the inheritor of Heidegger's approach, which he called *Destruktion* ('de-structuring'), and which Derrida calls deconstruction.

Alreadiness hints at our tuning to something else, which is a dance in which that something else is also, *already*, tuning to us. Indeed, there are some experiences in which it simply can't be said which attunement takes priority; which comes first, logically and chronologically. One of these is the common experience of beauty. We can learn a lot from it: let's go.

You are Being Tuned

We could talk about our current historical phase in many ways: entering an ecological era, learning how to cope with global warming, and so on. But what all these labels have in common is *transitioning to caring about nonhumans in a more conscious way*. This talk is about that, and as you'll see it's a lot stranger than it sounds.

In November 2015 I participated in *Ice Watch*, Icelandic-Danish artist Olafur Eliasson's installation outside the Panthéon in Paris. *Ice Watch* was designed to be seen by the delegates representing the nations of Earth in the COP21 negotiations, otherwise known as the global warming summit, which was held over thirteen days. Eliasson and I recorded a public dialogue about it in Copenhagen about one week before *Ice Watch* was installed, at the CPH:DOX film festival. One thousand people attended, eager to hear about ecology and art.

Ice Watch consisted of something like eighty tons of ice harvested from Greenland and shipped intact to Paris, where it was installed in twelve gigantic chunks, in a circle. From above, it readily resembled the little bars that stand for hours on a wristwatch. The chunks of ice were large enough to climb on to and sit in, or even lie in, and as there was no barrier protecting them, this is just exactly one of the things that people did. Part of the project was documentation of all the different ways in which you could access the ice. You could walk past it. You could ignore it. You could touch it. You could reach out towards it. You could talk about it. You could give a conference paper about it at a conference called *Façonner l'avenir*. You could sleep in it. This was especially easy once the sun had melted the ice enough for it to form smooth pockets and contours.

Part of the point of *Ice Watch* was an obvious visual gag: look, ice is melting and time is running out. But that was just the hook. What actually happened was much more interesting, and in a way that seriously stretched or went beyond prefabricated concepts, in a friendly and simple, yet deep way. Watches are things that humans read. But they are also things that flies land on, things that lizards ignore, things that the sun glints off. Dust settles on the glass shell of the front of the watch. A dust mite traverses the gigantic overpasses and caves on the underside of the watch between the watch and my wrist. And let's return to something I just said about *Ice Watch:* the sun melts it. The sun is also accessing the ice. The pavement is also accessing the ice. The climate of Paris is also accessing the ice.

And the ice was accessing us. It seemed to send out waves of cold, or suck our heat, whichever way around. This kind of access was how Eliasson was thinking about it – the encounter with *Ice Watch* is in a way a dialogue with ice blocks, not a one-way human conversation in a mirror that happens to be made of ice. We've been having that kind of conversation with nonhuman things for thousands of years. It's exactly the reason we are in this mess called global warming. And the climate factoids we hear on the news are echoed by much of the art that tries to address global warming and extinction. For example, several artists have compiled massive lists of lifeforms that are going extinct. But the risk here is of becoming just like those factoids: just a huge data dump. Art is important to understanding our relationship to nonhumans, to grasping an object-oriented ontological sense of our existence. Art fails in this regard when it tries to mimic the transmission of sheer quantities of data; it's not artful enough. This isn't just a matter of effective persuasion. As a matter of fact, that's the trouble with ecological data art. The aesthetic experience isn't really about data – it's about data-*ness,* the qualities we experience when we apprehend something. (As I mentioned earlier, data just means 'what is given', and isn't only about numbers and pie charts.) The aesthetic experience is about *solidarity* with what is given. It's a solidarity, a feeling of alreadiness, for no reason in particular, with no agenda in particular – like evolution, like the biosphere. There is no good reason to distinguish between nonhumans that are 'natural' and ones that are 'artificial', by which we mean made by humans. It just becomes too difficult to sustain such distinctions. Since, therefore, an artwork is itself a nonhuman being, this solidarity in the artistic realm is already solidarity with nonhumans, whether or not art is explicitly ecological. Ecologically explicit art is simply art that brings this solidarity with the nonhuman to the foreground.

Eliasson wanted to do something that was logically prior to collecting data, let alone spreading it around. To collect data, you have to be receptive. You need the right kind of data-gathering devices for your project. You need to care. A global warming scientist needs to care enough about global warming for her to set up the experiments that find out about it in the first place. In the beauty experience, there is some kind of mind-meld-like thing that takes place, where I can't tell whether it's me or the artwork that is causing the beauty experience: if I try to reduce it to the artwork or to me, I pretty much ruin it. This means, argues Kant, that the beauty experience is like the operating system on top of which all kinds of cool political apps are sitting, apps such as democracy. Nonviolently coexisting with a being that isn't you is a pretty good basis for that.

Since the being that isn't you is artwork, and so not necessarily human, or conscious, or sentient, or for that matter alive, we're talking about the possibility of being able to expand democracy, from within Kantian theory itself, to include nonhumans. Which is a pretty scary thought for some people – Kant himself, for example, which is one reason why he is so careful to police the magic ingredient, the beauty experience, that actually makes the rest of his philosophy work (like Heidegger, he pulls back on his own thought, not carrying it through to its potentially radical conclusions). Instead, he sort of introduces a little tiny drop of it to flavour the anthropocentric – and pretty much bourgeois – soup – too much and the soup is ruined; it ceases to nourish anthropocentric patriarchy. It's funny that the way to undermine Kant, as with Heidegger, is to take him more seriously than he takes himself, a tactic I've definitely inherited from deconstruction. And you do it by increasing the amount of the very ingredient that makes the soup so tasty.

When you encounter the beauty experience, it's not about anything in particular. If it really was a bowl of soup, you might want to eat it. Then you'd know what the thing was about: it was about future you, with a nice full belly. In a way, you would know the future of this entity, this object, this bowl of soup. But because beauty soup isn't for eating – because it's just this weird slightly telepathic mind meld between me and something that isn't me – you don't know the future. There is a strange not-yet quality built into how you access the thing you are finding beautiful. And because, from my point of view, beauty is sort of like having data, but the data isn't pointing at anything but itself – I'm just experiencing the givenness of data, of what is given. I'm experiencing the way data doesn't quite point directly at things. That's why you need scientists, right? They figure out patterns in data that hint at things. That's why science is statistical. That's why the sentence *humans are causing global warming* is actually not at all like *God created Earth in seven days*. You don't need to believe it in a firm sense. You can just accept it as pretty much true. You can be 98 per cent correct, and that's better than threatening me with torture unless I admit that you're completely right, because there's no other way for you to *be* right than to hit me until I agree.

I'm also experiencing something magic and mysterious about myself when I have that beauty experience. The ice is a sort of Pandora's box with an infinity within it. And so am I. It's that mouthfeel again. I'm experiencing the texture of cognitive or emotional or whatever phenomena. I'm experiencing *thinkfeel,* or better, since I can't tell whether it's about thinking or feeling but I know it's real and it's happening, it's *truthfeel* that I'm experiencing. It's as if I could magically see around the corners of myself to the part of me that's having the thoughts, because when I try normally, I just find another thought. I can't see all of my phenomenological style, how I manifest in a complete way, all at once – that total happening called 'me' is only accessible in slivers. Some people call this thing that keeps disappearing around the corner *consciousness,* Kant calls it the transcendental subject, but as we've seen, there's no particular reason to hold on to these concepts.

I magically see the unseeable aspects of a thing, including the thing called Tim Morton. I grasp the ungraspability of a thing. Which is another way of saying, I see the future, not the predictable one, but the unpredictable one. I see the possibility of having a future at all: I see *futurality.*

And in the case of the *Ice Watch* hunks of ice outside the Panthéon in Paris, Eliasson set this up so that you could see this future isn't a container for the ice block. It's coming directly out of the ice block itself – the ice block is creating the future. The ice really is a watch. And not a watch being set by humans. Or even better, it's a certain kind of time structure – it is a temporality structure. It allows you x and y and z kinds of past and future. This is the paradox. Futurality isn't some grey mist that is the same for a block of ice as it is for an excited proton underneath Geneva. Different objects, different futuralities. Unspeakableness or ungraspability can come in all kinds of flavours. It only sounds paradoxical because we're used to time and space being box-like containers in which things are sitting, where we place and try to contain them (no matter whether this effort is an illusion or not), whereas for Kant, and those who come after him, time is something posited, it's part of aesthetic experience, it's in front of things, ontologically, not an ocean in which they are floating, but a sort of liquid that pours out of a thing.

So we have to be careful what we humans design, because we are *literally* designing the future, and that future isn't in our idea of the thing, how we think it will be used and so on – that's just our access mode. The future emerges *directly from the objects we design.* Right now, many, many objects on Earth are designed according to a one-size-fits-all, very old, way past its sell-by-date temporality template. It's one we have inherited from Neolithic agriculture, that's how ancient it is. And it's the one that has given rise to industry with its fossil fuels and therefore to global warming and mass extinction. So designers should be careful what they design. Maybe they need to think at least on a number of different temporal scales when they design something. A plastic bag isn't just for humans. It's for seagulls to choke on, and now we can see that thanks to photographers such as Chris Jordan who photographs beings who get caught in the Pacific Garbage Vortex. A Styrofoam cup isn't just for coffee, it's for slowly being digested by soil bacteria for five hundred years. A nuclear device isn't just for your enemy. It's for beings 24,000 years from now. This Diet Coke isn't just for me. It's for my teeth and my stomach bacteria, and the latter may get slaughtered by the acids in there. This is why I created the concept of the *hyperobject* in my book *The Ecological Thought*. A hyperobject is a thing so vast in both temporal and spatial terms that we can only see slices of it at a time; hyperobjects come in and out of phase with human time; they end up 'contaminating' everything, if we find ourselves inside them (I call this phenomenon *viscosity*). Imagine *all the plastic bags in existence at all:* all of them, all that will ever exist, every-where. This heap of plastic bags is a hyper-object: it's an entity that is massively distributed in space and time in such a way that you obviously can only access small slices of it *at a time,* and in such a way that obviously transcends merely human access modes and scales.

Time Flows from Things

Everything emits time, not just humans. So when we talk about sustainability, what we're talking about mostly is maintaining some kind of human-scaled temporality frame, and this is necessarily at the expense of those other beings, and it's very likely we didn't factor them in at all. What exactly are we sustaining, if not the one-size-fits-all agricultural temporality pipe that has sucked all lifeforms into it like a vacuum cleaner, pretty much, over its 12, 500-year run? And in the end, which means already, designing stuff according to that template is going to damage humans as well, in a very obvious way, because of the unavoidable interconnectedness of everything we know and understand, and even everything we can't know or see, too. When the

Nazi propagandist Joseph Goebbels heard the word culture, he reached for his gun. When I hear the word *sustainability*, I reach for my sunscreen.

Everything we've been exploring in the last few pages occurs to you as ethical and political fallout from the Kantian beauty experience; as wonderfully open-ended, because the kind of futurality a piece of artwork opens up is unconditional: in other words, it doesn't have a rate at which it decays to nothing. You don't ever exhaust the meaning of a poem or a painting or a piece of music, and this is another way of saying that the artwork is a sort of gate through which you can glimpse the unconditioned futurality that is a possibility condition for predictable futures. Art is maybe one tiny corner in our highly (too highly) consciously designed – and way too utilitarian – social space where we allow things to do that to us. What would it look like if we allowed more and more things to have some kind of power over us?

This isn't quite the same thing as saying, along with the socialist William Morris, that functional things should be beautiful. That's because, on this view, things are just lumps without some nice decoration. But we're saying that there are no lumps. There are blocks of ice, humans, sunlight, the Panthéon, polar bears. The goal is not to take existing things such as sofas and houses and make them pretty in a way that working-class people can afford (for example). That kind of thing suffers from the same syndrome as sustainability: it's anthropocentrically scaled.

Likewise we can't do what we take to be the opposite, which is saying art is beautifully useless and if you can't appreciate it, that's your problem. Again, you are simply allowing its existing function for humans now – aka anthropocentric functioning – to be default. Art is a place where we get to see what it means to be human or whatever, which is why what I do is called humanities. But this isn't enough. One way this becomes obvious is when writing grant proposals that sound like pleading. Please, please don't hurt me, Mr Funding Source, I'm a sort of educated PR guy who is going to decorate this boring cupcake of scientism with these nice human-flavoured meaning-candies.

Realizing that there are lots of different temporality formats is basically what ecological awareness is. It's equivalent to acknowledging in a deep way the existence of beings that aren't you, with whom you coexist. Once you've done that, you can't unacknowledge it. There's no going back.

Enchantment: Causality as Magic

So far I haven't transgressed vanilla, basic Kantian Kant very much. Well, maybe the last bit. But now I'm going to push up some faders on the Kantian mixing desk that will add some more of the chilli flavours that he only allows in tiny droplets. Let's return to our poor grant applicant and indeed to our Arts and Crafts people, starting with William Morris. What is their language blocking? It's blocking the fact that art isn't just decoration. It's causal. *It does something to you.* The Platonists were right: art has an inherently disturbing (in a nice or not so nice way) effect, an effect that you don't intend and can therefore strictly be called *demonic*, in the sense that demons are the messengers of the gods: it's a message from somewhere else. Platonists accurately see the power of art, which is why some of them (such as Plato himself) want it to be banned or very heavily censored. An artwork does something to you, so if you think that only lifeforms can do things to you, this is a weird and challenging fact. If you think on top of this that only humans are empowered with the magical ability to impose meaning and temporality on things, then you are in for a bigger shock, because as I've argued, art emits time, which tells you something about how everything emits time. It's designing your future as much as you're designing its.

Kant only wants you to hear about 10 per cent of that, but it's a very important ingredient of the overall mix that you can't do without. But according to Kant, if you hear more than that, you are in danger of being *charmed or enchanted,* rather than experiencing beauty, and that, in his book, is not OK. It's OK to be wordlessly smitten by something, as long as you don't actually fall in love with it and ask it out on a date, or even worse, allow it to ask you out. He acknowledges that there is a mind meld, but only up to a point, and it really does have to do with how you're a human being imposing reality on things. So really, for Kant, the experience is coming from you, not the artwork. Mystery solved. Disenchantment in effect. We can relax. Kant didn't turn into Yoda. Which was on the cards, because he was fascinated with the paranormal (maybe in the same way homophobes are fascinated with homosexuality). He himself was entranced, but resented it or feared it. So while Kant had to allow the idea into his theory – mind melding with a nonhuman being is how the thing actually works – he did it in a contained way, not in a way that you'd notice, like a tiny subliminal droplet of Yodaness; a base to the soup whose ingredients you experience even if you don't know what they are.

By Yoda-ness I mean the actual Force, the one that eighteenth-century German physician Franz Anton Mesmer talked about, and which fascinated Kant: a sort of animal magnetism, a Force, argued Mesmer, was generated by lifeforms; it surrounds and penetrates them – it is like when Darth Vader makes a gripping movement with his hand, and not unlike how they used to mesmerize people with hand gestures, causing someone to believe they had been strangled – without touching them. Animal magnetism is to all intents and purposes identical with the Force of *Star Wars* fame; it is, as Obi Wan Kenobi observes, an 'energy field' that 'surrounds' and 'penetrates' us, and we can interact with it, with healing and destructive consequences.

That's the problem with art, isn't it? It sucks you in, whether or not it's telling the truth, it's so truthy, it's not right or wrong but still it's giving off this incredible truth vibe, it's pulling me into its tractor beam, in a moment it might say, 'I find your lack of faith disturbing, Tim,' and strangle me, at a distance. Art is telepathic – it's spooky action at a distance, which is also what Einstein didn't like about quantum theory. It makes things happen without needing to touch things. But art is also profoundly ambiguous:

we can't tell whether it's telling the truth or lying. Ambiguous *and* powerful at the same time for the same reasons.

Interlocked in the beauty experience, I might dissolve. The art thing might fit me so perfectly that I disappear. Turned up to 11, this My Bloody Valentine music will actually kill me. But I can't tear myself away from it. Resonating perfectly with the physical structure of this glass, an opera singer's voice causes it to explode. Maybe the beauty experience is like a little death warning light that goes off in my experiential space. Maybe beauty is death, in a way, just like the decadent aesthetes used to say. It's a reminder that things are fragile, because when one thing envelops another thing, that other thing might be overwhelmed or destroyed. Maybe when Oscar Wilde said, on his deathbed, 'This wallpaper and I are fighting a duel to the death; either it goes or I do,' he was telling the literal truth, and it only sounded like a joke because of our prejudices: the idea, for example, that appearances are superficial, while essences are fundamentally beyond appearance. The colour yellow shouldn't matter that much, we think. By the way, the wallpaper won.

So when I experience beauty, I am coexisting with at least one thing that isn't me, and doesn't have to be conscious or alive, in a noncoercive way, in which the possibility of death is vivid yet diluted and suspended. We coexist; we are in solidarity. I'm haunted, charmed, enchanted, under a spell, things could get out of control, but they won't, at least for now. The present moment collapses and I'm left with an uncertain, spectral futurality that is exactly what this chunk of ice happens to be. How it looks, how it feels, where it is sitting, its mass, its shape – all that, which we could call appearance, is the past. The ice chunk is a sort of train station in which past and future are sliding past one another, not touching, and what I mistakenly call present is a kind of relative motion between the two sliding trains of past and future. I call it *nowness* to differentiate it from a reified atomic 'present' that actually I don't think truly exists. A thing is exactly how the cookie crumbled, and how the cookie might crumble some more, and I get to coexist in this slightly sad, melancholic space where the crumbling happened, and where an uncertain future opens out. All cookies crumble, you know. That's why they can be cookies. Things are inherently fragile, they all contain a fatal flaw that allows them to exist, because they are always exactly what they are, yet never as they appear. They transcend all access modes but they are unique and distinct. The rift between being and appearing is ontological, in other words you can't point to it, it's intrinsic to a thing and it's why cookies can crumble. Even black holes evaporate.

And because it's not anthropocentrically scaled in particular, or ego-scaled in particular, when you have a conversation between beauty and disgust or ugliness, you can't delete it. It is a conversation between objects and abjection, which is a technical term some thinkers use to describe the functions of the body and the body's relation with its symbionts, against which the traditional Western human subject has learned to distinguish him- or herself. The more we know about objects from the OOO point of view, the more we realize that we can't cleanse them of their 'abject' qualities, because they aren't pristine, pure things, but pockmarked and pitted and oozing with all kinds of inconsistencies and anomalies – just like human beings. And because you're in truth space, you are having a conversation with actuality, even though it might not be your actuality or a human actuality. The artwork can't simply be a representation. The thing might have designs on you, to use the common English phrase. You feel this in the gravitational pull, the telepathic charm of the thing. And because of that, you are also having a conversation between having a purpose or a function and being beyond purpose or function, because a thing's function or purpose doesn't exhaust it. It just might not be your design or function or a human purpose in particular. Which is the same thing as saying you are having a conversation with utilitarianism, which is saying that you are having a conversation about happiness – whose happiness, and what kinds of happiness? Which means that you are having a conversation with what is probably something you think of as an inanimate object, like a block of ice, which means you are allowing yourself to be in a telepathic mind meld with something that stands for the worst possible fate of a human subject, being turned into an object. And because the truth space is truthy, not obviously truth as such, but saturated with truthiness data, you don't know whether it's true or not – the artwork is a lie that is telling the truth, or maybe it's a kind of truth that is lying. You are being telepathically seduced by a being that might be lying.

Actually *beings,* plural, so it's much, much worse, or better. Because there are so many more parts in the artwork than there is the whole of it, by definition, and by definition you're not allowed to discriminate either way – parts are more important than wholes, or vice versa, or one part is more important than the others – because that's finding a definite purpose, and the experience doesn't have that going for it. That would ruin it. This is due to that feature of

OOO theory which we've already met (and which I'm advocating here), in which there is always a multiplicity of parts that exceed the whole, rather than the whole swallowing the parts perfectly. An artwork is *subscended* by its parts. We've already been exploring the concept behind this term quite a bit. Recall what I've been arguing already: that wholes are bursting with their parts; in a basic but strange-seeming way, *wholes are less than the sum of their parts*.

Those parts are also little temporality structures, little train stations within train stations, multiple tractor beams pulling you in, multiple hypnotists. Possibly an infinite regress of them – you can't check. Because you know you can't reduce that blob of paint to something it isn't, such as its parts (like little crystals or whatever, or brushwork), you can't delete its causal pressure on you. You decide that free will is most definitely overrated and we are going to need some kind of chemical to coexist other than rights and sub-jecthood and citizenship and free will. Infinity portals beckoning. Maximum aesthetic suction and repulsion, like a horror movie superimposed on a porno. And you still can't stop looking. It's not transcendent beauty, but it's still beauty. Which is another way of saying, it's not your bourgeois subject's best friend, more like an anarchic revolutionary army of little squirming pieces crawling around and within that seemingly rigid and singular piece of cheese.

Kitsch is the subscendent part of beauty, ghosting official anthropocentrically scaled forms of beauty like a spectre. In a way, kitsch or disgust is the X-power (as in the X-Men) of beauty itself. Without it, beauty can't evolve.

You have gone crazy, maybe.

All those things that Kant tries to edit out are back in, without deleting the beauty experience as such. In fact, they are deeply how it works, what it can't do without.

No Design is Perfect

This isn't the normal utopian or left way of critiquing theories about our relationship to arts, or aesthetics. The normal way is to say that art is only a construct and doesn't really exist – for example, it's just a bourgeois human ideology reproduction mode based on inherited ideas of taste. But what I'm saying is that art is actually a tiny but still recognizable fragment of the kind of larger world, the mostly nonhuman world of influences and designs that go beyond us and violate our idea of who 'owns' what and who is running the show, such that causality seems to have something animistic or paranormal about it. It's not a glue that falsely fixes bourgeois dichotomies such as subject and object. I'm talking about a substance that is a dangerous toxin to anthropocentrism and mechanical causality theories and the law of noncontradiction and default utilitarianism. The law of non-contradiction, for example, is an important lynchpin of Western philosophy, but it's never been proved, only stated, first by Aristotle in section Gamma of the *Metaphysics*. It is easy to violate and also easy to draw up logical rules that allow for some things to be contradictory. Since ecological entities are contradictory by definition (they are made of all kinds of things that aren't them, they have vague fuzzy boundaries . . .), we had better permit ourselves to violate this supposed law, at least a bit.

Art only half works as a human-scaled bourgeois ideology reproduction device if you put just a tiny drop of it into the soup, and don't examine it too carefully or treat it as decoration. If you did, you would see all the subscendent little microbes squiggling around inside it, all of them trying to hypnotize you.

And this encounter with art tells us something about the encounter with any designed thing at all. Which is why you can sleep in an ice sculpture, which people were seen to do in Olafur Eliasson's *Ice Watch*. Or why tourists can take selfies in front of it, and there's nothing you can do about it. A thing is bursting with parts and scales and temporalities and sexualities, so a thing is never totally keyed to our taste or to a standard of good taste, but somehow that doesn't mean it's always definitely only ugly or that beauty and ugliness are false categories. It means that beauty is wild, spectral, haunting, irreducible, uncanny. And causal. Which means that the art versus craft or art versus design distinction breaks down, while leaving the difference between what a thing is for and its openness, its futurality, intact. 'Beautiful' is often said to be the opposite of 'useful'. It's held to be an unnecessary inconvenience, which is why so much of the modern world is so ugly. But beauty and usefulness *and* uselessness can't be separated at all. So every decision is a political one. Allowing a watch to be a landing strip for a fly. Allowing a plastic bag to be a bird murderer. Allowing a painting only to be seen by people who can afford the entrance fee. Living in a building designed to shunt dirty air somewhere else, where now we realize that *somewhere else* just means *nowhere else, because it's on the same planet*.

And irritatingly or wonderfully, this inbetweenness means you can never have the perfect design. Because interconnectedness doesn't mean that there is an obvious whole that obviously transcends its parts and is bigger and badder and better than the parts, and the parts are just components in the machine of the whole. A political system is also a designed thing, so this definitely affects what kinds of future politics we want. Including bunny rabbits means excluding diseases fatal to bunny rabbits. I mean this quite literally. Because of inter-dependence, when you take care of one entity or group of entities, another one (or more) is left out. Biocentric ecological philosophy is quite wrong to claim that the AIDS virus has the same right to exist as an AIDS patient. You have to choose. Obviously I'm going to choose the AIDS patient.

And because of the gap between being and appearing, to be a thing *at all* is to be deeply flawed; in order to exist at all you have to have an intrinsic invisible crack running all the way through you. So a network of things can't be perfect, and a thing on its own can't be perfect. You can't seal off the futurality, you can't stop time leaking out of things and mis-behaving, you can't reach the end of history, which now includes the history told by trees and geological layers and weather patterns. You just have to design your street knowing that, at some point, frogs are going to be crossing over it. At some point, it will be part of a geological stratum. At some point, a glint of light will reflect off a small puddle of water, blinding

a driver and killing a pedestrian. At some point . . .
The road is open, yet it's just this exact road, this
black tarmac thing with white stripes on it.

And this tells us something about design.
Humans can do it. But nonhumans also do it, all
the time. Think about evolution. It's design without a designer. And in a larger sense, nothing is
un-designed. There is no such thing as unformatted matter, waiting for someone to stamp a form
on it. That's an ecologically dangerous fantasy of
so-called Western civilization. In truth, anything
at all is in part a story about what happened to it.
My face has been designed by acne. A glass has been
designed by glass blowers and cutters. A black hole
has been designed by gravitational forces in a gigantic star. And in particular, things are definitely not
unformatted surfaces that can only be formatted by
human shaping or desire projection.

So the question is, with whom or what are we
going to team up, and what kinds of affordances are
we going to allow future beings, and how do we
allow the spooky suspension of violence, the possibly infinite vortices of pleasures and pains with us
and without us, like an eye that turns out to be a
bagful of hypnotic eyes, to happen without collapsing it so fast? Because we've been in the collapsing
business for quite a long time, we're really good at

it, and now it's not just killing the bees, it's even killing *us*. So instead, I let the subscendent beauty of the artwork hold me in its infinite tractor beams, like a bagful of hypnotic eyes. What to do with these uninvited guests? Let them stick around, I guess.

Actual beauty has a 'Christmas tree effect': there is a greasy pathway towards kitsch, in which we become aware of beauty's 'disgust fringe' – there's more subscendent beauty than normalized beauty can cope with. And when I talk about art, it is not just as a metaphor for us to understand the quality of existence. The subscendent nature of art means that ecological art that calls itself as such can't be about Sierra Club-style uplifting poster-type grandeur. It must include ugliness and disgust, and haunting weirdness, and a sense of unreality as much as of reality.

And in turn, ecological awareness can't just be pure and pristine and holy. Why can't there be an ecology for the rest of us? For those of us who don't want to go out camping in the fresh air, but would rather pull the covers over our heads and listen to weird goth music all morning? When can we start laughing, not just in a hale and hearty way, but with irony, a sense of the ridiculous, an excessive feeling of joy? What would an ecological joke sound like?

People are Strange When You're a Stranger

Things are exactly what they are, yet never as they seem, and this means that they are virtually indistinguishable from the beings we call *people*. A person is a being that veers in just this way. Once we start embracing difference not as rigid separation but as uncanny affinity, as I've been suggesting, we see that humans are more like nonhumans, and nonhumans are more like humans, than we like to think – and those two phrases do not quite add up. It is radically undecidable whether we are reducible to nonsentient, nonconscious, nonperson status – or whether things that aren't us, such as foxes or teacups, are reducible upwards to conventional personhood. I might be an android – this android might be a person: that's the best we can do. Deleting the hesitation by reducing either one to the other is what is called violence. If I decide you're just a machine, I can manipulate you exactly as I want. If I decide you're a person, and person means 'not a machine', then I can decide that other things are just machines by contrast, and manipulate them.

I am playing a tune called *myself* to which you are attuning, but which is itself attuned to you, so that we have an asymmetrical chiasmus between *myself* and me, between me and you.

We live in a world of tricksters. How we conduct ourselves in this world, the ethics of the trickster world, has to do with respecting that subjunctive, hesitant, might-be quality. It has to do with attunement. As I was saying before, in the context of thinking about life, attunement is a dance between completely becoming a thing, the absolute camouflage of pure dissolution (one kind of death) and perpetually warding off that thing (another kind of death), the mechanical repetition that establishes walls, such as cell walls. Between *I am that* and *me me me:* in other words, between being reducible to other stuff (I'm just a pile of atoms or mechanical components) and being totally different from other stuff (I'm a person, and only some beings get to be people). What is called life is more like an undead quivering between two types of death, a deviance that is intrinsic to how a thing maintains itself, or metastable as some like to say. Some things need to deviate to stay the same. Think of how a circle is how a line deviates from itself at every point, thanks to the seductive force of a number existing in a dimension perpendicular to that of the rational numbers (pi).

The Rothko Chapel, a non-denominational space

in central Houston, is one of Mark Rothko's final works, and it's located just behind where I live. It's a cool, dark space where the walls are adorned with gigantic versions of Rothko's characteristic abstract fields of vibrating colour, in a range of dark purples, blues and blacks.

My experience of showing guests around Rothko Chapel has provided me with beautiful examples of how, if you're scared or critical of art (perhaps you have been taught it's always a product of political oppression, or bourgeois sensibility, or a mystification designed to confuse you, or something like that), you find the sort of attunement that happens in there very uncomfortable. It's because you can't shrug it off or dismiss it as some unreal, ideological effect. Something is really happening – oh no, get me out of here! Because the Chapel is 'religious', you can't just put the paintings in a box with the label 'art'. Because the 'religious' quality is not specific, but more like a free-floating 'spirituality', you can't put that in a conceptual box either. Religion is turned into something like appreciating art; appreciating art is turned into something like spiritual contemplation. And those two transformations don't neatly map on to one another. So you can't dismiss what you're feeling as purely a social construct quite so easily.

The upshot? Some scholars have only lasted two

minutes in the Rothko Chapel. Some other friends, such as Björk and Arca, another musician friend, stay in there for ages and ages, soaking it up.

Why is this feeling of attunement scary for some? It's because it appears not just to be something they're in charge of, but something that's emanating from the paintings and the space itself. We attune to the gate-like rectangles of aubergine space, because they are already tuning to us, waiting, beckoning. A Rothko Chapel painting is a portal: just what might come through? Such a painting is a doorway for what Derrida calls *l'arrivant* (verb or noun?), the *future future*, the irreducible, unpredictable one. Philosophy, which is wonderment (hence horror, or eroticism, or anger, or laughter) in conceptual form, is an attunement to the way a thing is a portal for the future future. The love of wisdom implies that wisdom isn't fully here, at least not yet. Perhaps if it ever succeeded in teleporting down perfectly, it would cease to be philosophy. Thank heavens philosophy *isn't* wisdom. If it is, I want nothing to do with philosophy.

We might want to contain the aesthetic experience by framing it as 'art' in some predictable, preformatted sense. Going further, we might think art is a reflex of the commodity form, which would really help us to keep our suspicious distance:

heaven forbid we be seduced by anything. Art shows us how a disturbingly ambiguous pretence is woven into aesthetic experience: wonderment is based on the capacity to be deceived. The more we are OK with being lied to, the wiser we might become. 'Ever get the feeling you've been cheated?' (John Lydon, aka Johnny Rotten, once said onstage during a Sex Pistols concert). So perhaps we could dismiss a Rothko painting, as art critic Brian O'Doherty does in his famous essay on the commodification of art space, the dreaded 'white cube' of the contemporary gallery, now replicated in a million minimalist townhome interiors.

We want art to make us sure that we aren't being conned or ripped off or pitched to or prostituted or sold to: tuned. But this is exactly what art can't do. Art theory in modernity tends to want to distinguish art from conning or selling or ripping off, and from the dreaded status of 'object'; and this results in art's confinement to a tiny experiential region, sophisticated beyond sophistication, purer than the white cube purity of the philistine buyer and owner, hanging on the white walls but above anything that smacks of gross consumerism.

As anyone who is vaguely familiar with the very highstakes and high-priced art industry will attest, this abstinence (and abstinence from abstinence) is exactly the top level of consumer space: the self-reflexive, 'Romantic' mode of bohemian consumerism, in which we are all caught. Think of how we all like to say we no longer follow *fashion*, but instead select our very own *style*. One style can then be sampling everyone else's style, and this can seem as if you are floating above everyone else, the poor fools, trapped in consumerism. Yet this performance, which we could call 'I Am Not a Consumer', is the *ultimate* consumerist performance. O'Doherty has no time for what he thinks is the abstracting, reifying 'Eye' induced by the white cube space itself. But he has even less time for the poor corporeal 'Spectator', the comical, humiliated body dragged around by this eye. O'Doherty is saying that the way art galleries are set up, we are moved around them in a passive way, watching ourselves from an abstract distance. This means that being passive is bad, because being passive means being an object, which means not being a subject. Heaven forbid that we become an object, heaven forbid that we ever become passive – that would be a fate worse than death.

Attunement is the feeling of an object's power over me – I am being dragged by its tractor beam into its orbit. And yet we are told that we are not to be manipulated. We write essays such as *Inside*

the White Cube about how white cube spaces inevit-
ably seduce us all – except for me, the narrator of the
white cube essay, and you, the sophisticated reader
whom the essay is interpellating, rising above it all,
exiting the poor beastly body and the abject world
of objects, like the Neoplatonic soul transcending
the body. 'Obey your thirst' (advertisement for the
soft drink Sprite, 1990s) has no effect on us. Everyone gets conned by objectification, except for me,
the one who writes the sentence *Everyone gets conned
by objectification*. All sentences are ideological, except
for the sentence *All sentences are ideological*. Can you
see how this works?

Critique mode is the mode of the pleasure of no-
pleasure, the sadistic purity of washing your hands
of the crime of being seduced, as if *detuning* were
about exiting attunement space rather than what
really happens, which is only *retuning*. In this mode,
the worst thing that could happen is that you could
make or enjoy kitsch. Happily, children have never
heard of such things. My son Simon tells me that if
you cross your eyes and stare at a Rothko painting
just so, the red lines will start to vibrate and float
towards you, and you will feel nauseous and giddy –
and that these are exciting, oddly pleasant sensations,
like spinning in a swivel chair. Apparently the paintings aren't just commodities sitting primly in a shop

window. Apparently they even exceed their human-keyed 'use value'. For O'Doherty, the best kind of art, which he calls postmodern, is an endless conversation between (human) subjects about what good art might be, as if tuning up were not part of the orchestral performance – a myth rapidly dispelled by the first few seconds of 'Sgt. Pepper's Lonely Hearts Club Band'. Actually letting yourself enjoy a thing is pleasurably avoided. And yet to a six-year-old child, it's obvious that Rothko is trying to blow your mind.

Art sprays out charismatic causality despite us. And unlike a lot of things in our current world, and within limited parameters (sophistication, taste, cost), we still let it in. Art is a realm of passion for no reason: I just like this particular shade of blue, I want you to feel the weight of this metal toe, come in to this installation, look, peer through the curtain. The time of novels is the time of lust – the first novels were necessarily pornography (Arentino). So when we talk about art, we are talking in the region of love and desire, those unsteady, uneasy, wavering partners.

Let us widen our gaze from the artwork to a more general description of this region. Love is not straight, because reality is not straight. Everywhere, there are curves and bends, things veer.

Per-ver-sion. En-vir-onment. These terms come

from the verb *to veer*. To veer, to swerve towards: am I choosing to do it? Or am I being pulled? Free will is overrated. I do not make decisions outside the universe and then plunge in, like an Olympic diver. I am already in. I am like a mermaid, constantly pulled and pulling, pushed and pushing, flicked and flicking, turned and opened, moving with the current, pushing away with the force I can muster. An environment is not a neutral empty box, but an ocean filled with currents and surges. It environs. It veers around, making me giddy. An aesthetic wormhole, bending the terrestrial and ecological into the cosmological. The torsion of deep space, beaming into the cold water of this stream like bent light, the stream where I was caught by the fish I was catching a few pages ago.

Spacetime as such is a bending, a curvature. It isn't correct to say that spacetime is first flat, then distorted by objects. Objects directly *are* the distortion of spacetime: spacetime is the distortive force field that emanates from them. Curvature, lumps and bumps, a strange plenitude everywhere, no dead air. Spacetime isn't a flat blank sheet that gets disturbed. Spacetime is disturbance. A disturbing lens of matter-energy, we see as much as we can see, always less than all, through the convex kaleidoscope of spacetime. A thing is dappled with time.

But not a lump coated with time, improved by the makeup of motion. Better: a thing *is* this temporal dappling.

The nineteenth-century writer John Ruskin was a great scholar of architecture who argued that the modern tendency to want to clean old buildings, very much in effect today, was a sacrilegious erasure of what he liked to call *the stain of time*. In a sense Ruskin was aiming at something like an ontological redescription of things: to remove the time stain is to harm the actual thing, because a thing *actually is* this temporal staining. To want to cleanse a building of what is taken to be a supplementary stain is to assume that a thing underlies its appearance, the old default substance ontology. To allow things to get dirty is to allow that things are not at war with time. Further still, the 'dirty' Sistine Chapel ceiling painted by Michelangelo is similar today to how it would have been seen in flickering candlelight.

Newton's world is a realm of straight love, instant beams of gravity that are God's love, everywhere, all at once, outside time, the omnipresent force of an omniscient being acting on static extensional lumps, exciting them, pushing and pulling them around like cattle.

We do not live in Newton's world.

Einstein's world is a realm of perverse desire,

invisible ripples of gravity waves that make up spacetime, the invisible ocean in which the stars float submerged. We love the dead. We love fantasies. Do they love us back? We are pulled towards them and as this happens, time expands and shrinks like a polymer. No God could be omniscient in such a world, where time is an irreducible property of things, part of the liquid that jets out of a thing, undulating. There are parts of the universe that an observer will never be able to check. They are real. Things happen there. But some observers will never know *where* they are happening, or *when* they are happening. Some people in the universe will never know you are reading this, because they never *can* know. Just as you won't be able to know them.

In a universe governed by the speed of light, parts are hidden, withdrawn, obscure. The dark Dantean forest of the Universe, an underwater forest of rippling weeds. You should find this idea extremely comforting. It means that you cannot be omnipresent or omniscient. It means that you cannot look down on the poor suffering beings of the universe from a position outside time, and smile sadistically at their pain, a smile we often call pity. This is what we sometimes call the abstract gaze of the Enlightenment, that period in the early history of modern Europe and America in which universal values were articulated, unfortunately at the expense of urgent particularities such as race, class and gender. Many artworks of this period, such as C. F. Volney's *The Ruins of Empires* or Shelley's *Queen Mab,* are staged from precisely this position outside of the universe as a way to judge it.

Each entity in Einstein's universe is like the veering turbulence in a stream, a *world tube* or vortex that cannot know all. There is a darkness that cannot be dispelled.

Consider now the even stranger, and even more accurate, description of things we call quantum theory. In quantum theory, the binary between moving and staying still – between a certain concept of *verb* and *noun,* or between a certain concept of *object* and *quality* – becomes impossible to sustain. Objects isolated as much as possible from other objects still vibrate without being pushed, that is to say, without being subject to mechanical causation.

The idea that I'm outside the world, looking in, wondering which choice to make, is the ethical equivalent of the substance ontology that separates being from appearance with firewalls and fungicides. But the traditionalist 'conservative' versions of this line of thought, called 'environmentalism', also try to contain wavering, the hesitation filled with the vibrations of attunement. It's called environmentalism, but it's not en-vir-onmental enough.

And this isn't surprising, because 'traditional' agrilogistics ends up as our current version, so that there is a line from the notion of the guiding weight of tradition to the play of infinite (human) freedom and 'choice'. The aesthetic dimension is commonly imagined as a special glue that sticks these two poles together, by allowing humans to impose the proper form, to adapt their world perfectly to their require-ments. But this is not how it works. We have seen that this dimension is deeply entwined with things as such, not with (human) formatting. There is a certain courage of letting yourself fall asleep and allowing dreams to come, which resembles the courage of allowing art to affect you. Hallucinatory phantasms are a condition of possibility for seeing anything at all. Hearing is a chiasmic crisscross between sounds emitted by my ear and pressure waves perturbing the ear's liquids from the outside. The not-me beckons, making me hesitate.

The Uncanny Valley

The word for *familiar and strange at the same time is uncanny*. It's not exactly *otherness* that we are working with here. Ethics and politics might not be about tolerating, appreciating or accepting otherness. Ethics and politics might be about tolerating, appreciating or accepting *strangeness*, which boils down to *ambiguity*: how things can appear to be oscillating between familiar and strange, for example.

Doesn't appreciating art have to do with allowing things to be ambiguous? It's not just that there are all kinds of paintings and sculptures and books and pieces of music in this world, with all kinds of cultures to do with how these things are made, received and interpreted (and so on). What it is, and this is the most basic thing perhaps, is that you have no idea what this artwork will 'say' to you next: it's especially obvious when you've lived with a favourite piece for several years.

Deeper still, there is something strange that happens in the appreciation of art, which many philosophers have found disturbing. It's disturbing how the experience of relating to art, for example, makes it difficult – sometimes impossible – to sustain the valley across which we see other entities as 'other'. Let's see how. It's pretty obvious that art has an effect on me, and this effect is to a large extent unbidden: I didn't ask for it, which is part of the fun. I had no idea I could be affected in precisely *this* way. My whole sense of what 'affect' means has been transformed by this artwork – and so on. When I love an artwork, it is as if I am in some strange kind of mind meld with it, something like telepathy, even though I 'know very well' (or do I?) that this thing I'm appreciating isn't conscious, isn't sentient, isn't even alive. I am experiencing unknown effects on me coming from something that I am caught up with in such a way that I can't tell who 'started it' – am I just imposing my concepts of beauty on to any old thing, or is this thing totally overpowering me? The real feeling of experiencing what we sometimes call beauty is neither about our putting a label on to things, nor of our being absolutely inert. Instead it's like finding something in me that isn't me: there is a feeling in my inner space that I didn't cook up myself, and it seems to be sent to me from this 'object' over there on the gallery wall, but when I try to find out exactly where this feeling is and what it is about the thing, or about me, that is the reason why I'm having this feeling, I can't isolate it without ruining what precisely is beautiful about it.

What is the difference between *tolerate* and *appreciate*? It is all about this theme of coexisting. *Tolerate* means that within my conceptual reference frame, I allow something to exist, even though my frame doesn't really allow it. *Appreciate* means that I just admire it, no matter what my reference frame is.

That's why we use the term *appreciate* to talk about art. No one says 'I really tolerated that Beethoven string quartet' in a positive way. But you can easily say 'I really appreciated that disco tune' and people will know that you mean something positive.

When you think about it like this, you can see why being able to *appreciate* ambiguity is at the basis of being ecological. And do you know what this means? Your indifference to ecological things is exactly the sort of place where you will find the right kind of ecological feeling. This is one big reason why deleting the indifference too aggressively and too fast, by being preachy, doesn't help at all. *You don't know why you should care*: isn't that what we are all feeling when we experience something beautiful? How come this chord sequence is making tears run down my face?

Reasons for being nice to other lifeforms abound, but around them there is a ghostly penumbra of feelings of appreciating them for no reason at all. Just loving something never has a great reason attached to it. If you can list all the reasons why you 'should' love this particular person, you are probably not in love. If you have no idea, you might be nearer the mark. This ambiguous spectral aesthetic halo around ethical decisions doesn't tell us how to act, or even whether or not to act. It has a 'passive' quality about it, as if even our distinction between *active* and *passive* were not that thin and rigid, and that what is often meant by *passive* is in fact the penumbra we are talking about. Is how you relate to a beautiful artwork active or passive? You certainly don't want to eat it, because that would get rid of it, and you like it. But it's not clobbering you either. It's affecting you, but in a nonviolent way.

X-Ecology

There is a sort of ethical and political Uncanny Valley too. What happens when we let the spectres out of that Valley, the spectres that haunt us with supposedly divergent versions of what counts as human? What happens when it becomes an ethical-political Spectral Plain?

When care is ramped up, stripped down, simplified in order to boost its energy – so we think – it loses some very precious qualities. I once came across a beautiful encapsulation of the issue when I was in Boulder, and saw a calligraphy by a Buddhist teacher called Ösel Tendzin in the hallway of my friend Diane's house. With a huge brush, he had drawn two words, disconnected yet connected: CARE LESS. That summed it up. In this understanding, seeming 'careless' might blend into a beautiful encapsulation of the issue, in which seeming 'care-less' might blend into being 'carefree', and where some modes of 'care' might end up being too heavy-handed. I'm not saying you can save Earth by playing videogames on the couch. I'm saying that being ecological isn't the same as being religious in a tight way, even though it isn't the same as being an atheist in a tight way either – because that's just upside-down religion. Since organized religion is an agricultural-age way for agricultural society to understand itself, it is riddled with the kinds of bug that have helped to destroy Earth. 'Store up your treasure in heaven' (as Jesus advises) means you don't need to worry so much about what happens down here, because it's less real and less important. Heidegger observed that Christianity was Platonism for the masses. I'm observing that, historically speaking at least, Platon-ism is Neolithic theism for the educated elite.

It's the same as how truthiness haunts truth. You could imagine this ambiguous care/less care/free quality as a spectre, like the spectres on the Spectral Plain, a sort of ethical spectre. It weirdly shadows and doubles and undermines and reinforces it. In short, it's a bit of a problem: but trying to shave this penumbra off and achieve a more smooth-looking form of care creates bigger problems. The care / less-ness of indifference haunts care. But if we exorcise that ghost, we're back to survival for the sake of survival, and how's that been working out so far for life on this planet? We are so busy, and our current neoliberal machinations are just the latest upgrade to a busy, busy mentality that has been gripping us since 10,000 BCE. The one emotion we love to hate in the media is apathy.

I recall, as a proud (?) member of Generation X, how we were being told we didn't care enough about anything through the 1990s. It's funny, because as I looked around as the twenty-something me, I saw a lot of care in the 'civilized' world: people getting depressed by modern working conditions, people going into despair about environmental issues, nuclear families going subatomic, teenage years now extending to the age of thirty. Against the happy-happy enforcement of care, seeming a bit slack (a term we now use as Richard Linklater's film *Slacker* uses it) was a wonderfully refreshing stance. I guess we could distinguish between claustrophobic, plastic forms of care, and more aerated, flexible ones.

I love being an X-er. The advertising, PR-type people who come up with these labels didn't know what label to slap on us, because we weren't behaving as we should. It's interesting if you are in the lineages of deconstructive philosophy as I am (Heidegger, Derrida and on). When Heidegger writes the word *Being* he puts it under a letter X, a gesture that Derrida calls *putting under erasure*. You can't say *Being* positively with a straight face, it makes Being look all bloated and solid like a huge blank bar of bland soap.

The CARE/LESS is the halo of care, its aura. When it gets hand-wringing, ecological talk retains a strong smell of the agricultural-age machinating that got us into this mess – it's that huge blank bar of bland soap again. I don't want to live in the world that kind of machinating would bring about. It would make the ways in which this current world sucks (to use a Gen-X term) look like the best thing that ever happened to anyone. I'm talking about a world based on greater and greater efficiency, greater and greater control of energy. You can see this is how some people think about an ecological society. Instead, I think it's a world in which we can be so much more generous and creative than we've ever been, so much less 'caring' in that way that is hostile to actual lifeforms: survival mode.

Plastic care, stripped down and efficient, is highly toxic, especially when you scale it up to Earth magnitude and operate like that for 12,500 years. What is required instead is *playful care*. This doesn't mean care that is cynical. We actually have quite a lot of that: big corporations now enforce 'fun' in a most coercive manner. You are supposed to sing company songs or participate in collective team-building activities, or use videogame-like interfaces for working ('gamification'). We need something like the inverse, something like a *playful seriousness*. This mode would have a slight smile on its face, knowing that all solutions are flawed in some way. Expanded care, care with the care/less halo, is more likely to include more lifeforms under its umbrella, because it is less focused on sheer survival. The contrast we sometimes draw between selfishness and altruism is made from within a streamlined care outlook. You think there is a self and that therefore it needs protecting and boosting, and that caring for things that aren't the self would therefore involve some almost impossible to imagine emptying of the self, which in some agricultural-age religious domains is called *kenosis,* the Greek for 'emptying'. That doesn't sound fun and it doesn't even sound possible. It's a set-up. It's like how people are scornful about Buddhism – how can you desire to get rid of desire?

If I don't get behind this expanded care idea, then really, this whole book has been a big waste of time. Because while I've been letting myself off the hook and not yelling factoids at you, secretly I'm not letting *you* off the hook and secretly I'm preaching to you, trying to convert you in a sneakier way.

I'm machinating, but under the radar. That would mean that the whole way I wrote this was actually the opposite of playful seriousness: it was serious playfulness, goal-directed and 'fun'. I'd be trying to persuade you, and I think believing means holding on for dear life, and this is just a sales pitch.

So, in fact, I meant it all along, dear reader. I meant it when I said you didn't need to delete your indifference. You are quite right. You work so hard and you get so little in return, you have to smile relentlessly at work, you have to be your own paparazzo and upload a selfie to Facebook every five minutes, you have to 'Like' (that button) the right sorts of thing. In Freudian terms, your poor little ego is under attack from both sides, from the impulses of the id and the demands of the superego, both irrational and often superimposed, in our culture of 'repressive desublimation'. And now I'm asking you to get all frantic about polar bears too? On top of everything else? So much frantic clicking, so much preening of exactly the right thing to say, a goal whose posts change every day, like the statistics. The thing about the superego is, it's impossible to fulfil its demands. Is it a feature of our psyches or a bug? Whatever the case, it's been inflamed by agricultural-age religion and its current ecological incarnation is therefore, however well meaning, a way of perfuming ecology space with exactly the wrong smell: the smell of busy, busy, zealous, industrious, 'just keep swimming, just keep swimming' intensity.

Perhaps some of us care in all the wrong ways – too aggressively, too melancholically, too violently. Heidegger argues that even indifference is a form of care. Perhaps indifference itself is pointing to a way to care for humans and nonhumans in a less violent way – simply allowing them to exist, like pieces of paper in your hand, like a story you might appreciate – or not – for no reason.

Inconclusive in Conclusion

Being ecological is like being a teacher. When you first start teaching, you try so hard to teach that it becomes excruciating. You want your students to like you. You want to like them. You don't want to feel this excruciating feeling that you yourself are generating by trying so hard. You start to work with aggression (or you quit). You realize that you are a channel for your and your students' negative as well as positive feelings, and your job is to hold those feelings for the students' benefit. Then you wonder why you are trying so hard, and maybe you start to let go. You begin to trust. You begin to realize that you are a teacher, no matter what, because at least one other person knows you're their teacher.

You can relax into that. It's the same when you're a parent. You spend some time trying desperately to *be* a parent. And then once you realize that you just are a parent, you can relax. At least someone knows you're their parent.

You are a fully embodied being who has never been separated from other biological beings both inside and outside your body, not for one second. You are sensitively attuned to everything happening in your world, which is why you end up blocking some of it, because you are afraid the stimulation might be too intense. You have an idea that there is an inside and an outside of yourself, and perhaps this is the deepest way in which you start to think that being ecological involves some massive change.

Snared in the urgency of ecological awareness and the horror of extinction and global warming, it's so incredibly difficult to miss this key point. I can't tell you how many environmentalist conferences I've been to where the ending atmosphere had to do with some kind of fist-clenching, jaw-clenching desperation to be or do something totally different. What a set-up – once you've established this totally different space, you are already separated from it by a gigantic chasm, and being right or smart in this kind of world means showing yourself and everyone how deep and wide this chasm is. You've just made sure that you are never going to be ecological. The one thing that could help gets drowned out by the fear of the intensity of our reactions to the data input (oceans acidifying! Climate warming! Species going extinct!).

But you are already a symbiotic being entangled with other symbiotic beings. The problem with ecological awareness and action isn't that it's horribly difficult. It's that it's too easy. You are breathing air, your bacterial microbiome is humming away, evolution is silently unfolding in the background. Somewhere, a bird is singing and clouds pass overhead. You stop reading this book and look around you.

You don't have to *be* ecological. Because you *are* ecological.